LORD, TEACH US TO PRAY

LORD, TEACH US TO PRAY

The Ultimate Request Every Disciple Should Make

Dr. Jimmy Knott
with Linda Knott

Foreword by Dr. Jim Henry

XULON PRESS

Xulon Press
2301 Lucien Way #415
Maitland, FL 32751
407.339.4217
www.xulonpress.com

Scripture quotations taken from the English Standard Version (ESV). Copyright © 2001 by Crossway, a publishing ministry of Good News Publishers. Used by permission. All rights reserved.

Printed in the United States of America.

ISBN-13: 978-1-54565-688-4

DEDICATION

To Dr. Jim Henry and Dr. David Uth who provided me fantastic leadership and opportunity to grow in my journey with Christ. Both modeled the importance of prayer. Thanks to both of you.

PRAISE FOR
LORD, TEACH US TO PRAY

Jimmy has given us a simple and practical look at prayer. Through his book, he shares the story of his life and what he has learned about prayer through some of the most difficult circumstances one could ever go through. He gives us an opportunity to see very personal lessons he has learned through some of the most incredible trials. I have served with Jimmy for over 13 years and have watched God do so much in his life. I am thankful that he took the time to share with us the difference prayer has made in his journey with God. As you will come to understand from this book, you don't really learn to pray by simply reading pages in a book, but by living a life yielded in surrender to God.

Dr. David Uth

Senior Pastor, First Baptist Orlando

Jimmy Knott has written a classic on the topic of prayer. This book contains many helpful tools to develop a more consistent and meaningful connection with God. The material is Biblical, practical and guaranteed to help people in their journey to a more fulfilling prayer life.

Pat Williams

Orlando Magic co-founder and senior vice president

Author of CHARACTER CARVED IN STONE

Lord, Teach Us to Pray is an outstanding book in large part because the author, Jimmy Knott, lives what he encourages us to do . . . become men and women of prayer. It is practical, compelling and clear. A more effective prayer life and deeper intimacy are the by-product of engaging in this wonderful book. I heartily recommend it!

Howard Dayton

Founder, Compass-Finances God's Way

I loved Jimmy Knott's newest book on prayer. Jimmy is an outstanding leader and teacher and has impacted a large number of people for decades. His devotion to being a daily disciple of Jesus continues to be an ongoing inspiration for many people. When I initially asked Jimmy why he had written this book, he told me because it was the one spiritual practice that he has struggled with most. I immediately knew this book would impact others because it was written from the 'place' that all of us can identify with. I especially love the chapter of praying through your problems. Few books on prayer address this issue as well as this does. Get this book. Read this book. Pray through this book.

David Loveless

Discipleship & Groups, First Baptist Orlando

Jimmy Knott has been a consistent disciple of Christ for the 30+ years I have known him. I have been personally affected by his desire to help others grow in their walk for Christ. The Biblical disciplines he has taught me have been invaluable, none more important than regular time in God's word and prayer. I wish I had had this thoughtful yet practical book through the ups and downs of life over those past 30 years, yet I am thrilled to have it now! I especially liked how Jimmy boldly tackles some important questions about prayer; such as, does God answer my prayer, how does God hear me, does God really care about my problems, and many more. I want my children and grandchildren to read Jimmy's book. I know it will be an important resource in their desire to grow a stronger and more fulfilled relationship with Jesus Christ.

Jim Cumbee, JD, MBA

Tennessee Supreme Court Rule 31 Listed

General Civil Mediator

Jimmy Knott is a disciple maker. In this book, come join him and learn to move your prayer life from the ordinary to the extraordinary with this study of why, what and how in talking and listening to God. My number one goal each year is to be in an intimate relationship with God, and grow as a Christ follower. This book enriches that journey. The chapter on "putting it all together" is a go-to guide that demonstrates how to daily live what Christ taught when the disciples asked, "Lord teach us to pray."

Dr. Stephen C. Vogt
CEO BioPlus Specialty Pharmacy
Trustee, First Baptist Orlando

If you're looking for a guide on how to pray, go no further than "Lord, Teach Us to Pray." Practical, insightful, and intuitive are just a few of the words that describe Dr. Knott's guide to understanding and applying prayer in your life. If you want to become an instrument of God and find His purpose for you in life, this book is where you should start.

Dr. Philip G. Lilly
Executive Pastor/Author
First Baptist Church, St. Petersburg, FL

Blessed to be a 40-year friend of Jimmy Knott. In "Lord, Teach Us to Pray" I find expressions of love and practice from a man who has learned to pray! Jimmy has guided men like me as they entered and matured in vocational ministry, encouraging devotion and pushing for effectiveness.

In this book, Jimmy takes us back to the basics of prayer while reminding us of the rich depths of blessing God opens to us as He invites us into His throne room. Thanks, Jimmy, for bringing us back home to our spiritual roots.

Michael C. Cummings
Serve Pastor
First Baptist Church, Charlotte, NC

Pastor Jimmy is what I call WISE. He has learned through many significant life experiences what the power of prayer is. When someone has walked with Christ as Pastor Jimmy has we would also be WISE to listen to him. Prayer Matters! Pastor Jimmy will help you see just how much!

Dr. Ben Rall
Achieve Wellness Founder and Author of "Moving from Corporate Wellness to Cooperate Wellness"
Team Chiropractor for the 2012 Olympics for USA wrestling, judo and weightlifting

For nearly 40 years I have had the privilege of sitting under Jimmy Knott's teaching, serving alongside him in ministry, or simply doing life with his family. During this entire time, I have been blessed by his genuine obedience to teaching God's Word, and to training disciples for Jesus Christ. This is more than a book—it is a compelling challenge and practical guide to develop the spiritual discipline of prayer. I needed to read this and to have a renewed focus on prayer. The hustle and bustle of life often derails our prayer life—I am grateful for a friend and leader like Jimmy Knott who has brought me back to the essential part of my relationship with Christ.

Larry Taylor
Headmaster, Prestonwood Christian Academy, Plano, TX

Jimmy Knott has taken on a topic that nearly every Christian struggles with at one time or another—Prayer! In his book "Lord, Teach Us to Pray", Dr. Knott helps you understand the real purpose of prayer and then gives you a strategy to make your prayer life more meaningful and more successful. This book comes straight from the heart of a teacher and you won't want to miss it!

Robert Story
Digital Marketing Strategist, Oracle Corporation

One night when I was about twelve years old, I remember waking up from a light slumber to the gentle sound of you praying over me. I kept my eyes closed and just listened. Your voice was so comforting, and I could truly feel the presence of the Holy Spirit. You taught me that night, and on many other occasions, the value of a strong prayer life. Today, I pray with my own children in the firm belief that they in turn learn the importance of talking with God. Thank you, Dad, for being such an amazing father, teacher, coach and friend. I love you and I am so proud to call you Dad!

Stephanie L. Cook
Partner, ShuffieldLowman, Attorneys and Advisors
Orlando Office

TABLE OF CONTENTS

ACKNOWLEDGMENTS

Few things of significance are accomplished in life that aren't a team effort. That is true in the writing of this book. The people who get you to the finish line are of utmost importance. I'd like to offer my deepest gratitude to the following people for joining me in this journey:

First and foremost, to my God and Savior Jesus Christ and His unending patience with me and my prayer life.

To my wife, Linda, for her exemplary prayer life, her constant encouragement, and her contribution to this book.

To all my editors, led by my wife, Linda. I wrote some copy that was unreadable. Your wisdom, expertise, and effort made it palatable.

To my youngest son, Justin, and his wonderful wife, Kelley, for their professional expertise with the production of the book in social media

& content marketing. If you ever have social media & marketing needs, they are awesome (contact Justin@Intrepy.com or visit Intrepy.com).

To First Baptist Orlando Communications team, especially Sarah Stephens. They were so helpful with edits and design.

To Donna George, my long-time Executive Assistant, for her patience, diligence, and joyful spirit in managing this project.

To Don Newman and the entire Xulon Publishing Team who guided me all the way to upload and print. They are the best! It was truly an honor to publish with you again. You honor Jesus with the ministry you do, and it shows.

Last, but not least, to you the reader, for your willingness to pick up this book and give the time to read it. I am honored you chose to do so. My prayer is it will be an encouragement and provide you with a plan to improve your prayer life.

FOREWORD BY DR. JIM HENRY

I heard about a man hired to paint white lines along the highway. The first day he painted 10 miles. The boss was so impressed that he promised a raise if he could keep up the pace. But the next day he only did 5 miles, and the third day only one mile. He was fired. As he walked away he was heard to say, "It wasn't my fault. I kept getting farther away from the can." All of us know that the source of power is found in staying connected with the power source, our Lord Jesus Christ. Yet, we like followers of Jesus through the years struggle with prayer. We know that the very essence of a significant daily life is connected directly to the awareness of His presence developed through fellowship with Him in meditation and prayer.

If you have followed Jesus a long time your prayer life may have consisted with the first memory of prayer shared at the dinner table: "God is great, God is good, let us thank Him for our food." When we memorized the bedtime prayer, "Now I lay me down to sleep, I pray the Lord my soul will keep, and if I die before I wake, I pray the Lord my soul will take." As an athlete, you may have knelt with teammates before or after an athletic event and prayed the Lord's prayer. Perhaps a crisis, a rigid school exam, an illness or a doctor's report caused you to pray a simple, "Lord, help me!" As we mature in our walk with Christ, we begin to yearn for a deeper intimacy with Him. We heard it said that our spiritual life will never rise above the level of our prayer life. So, we scramble to take time to pray, to learn how to pray: We try to copy the examples of great men and women who are or were prayer warriors. We attend seminars and hear sermons on prayer. We read about prayer. I have at least 69 books on prayer in my library and I have a folder full of hundreds of sermons, illustrations, instructions, and insights about prayer. I hunger to get closer to my Lord, but at times, I'm painfully aware that I am at the elementary level in the school of prayer.

Then, Jimmy asked me to write this foreword. I didn't feel qualified, but I asked for the manuscript. I figured it would be just another in a profusion of material on the subject. To my great joy I found it to be the most complete handbook on prayer I've ever read. I thought I would read a few chapters periodically and get around eventually to finishing it. I couldn't put it down! I read it straight through and thought, "I wish I had this in my hands years ago." Jimmy has exercised his spiritual gifts of teaching and organization to put this material in a cohesive, readable, and biblically sound format. If you are desiring a closer walk with God, or teaching, or preaching, this book is a mother lode of gold for you individually or for a group.

Thanks, Jimmy. You have done a good thing to assist us in drawing near to the One who desires to listen to us and to talk with us. He told us we "ought always to pray and not to faint." We say with the early disciples, "Lord, teach us to pray." This significant work will be a nest egg of information and instruction to do just that. . . and help you paint life in straight lines by keeping close to THE SOURCE.

INTRODUCTION

When S. D. Gordon stated, "Prayer is not the only thing, but it is the chief thing,"[1] he was stating a truth most Christians were yet to understand. One day a disciple of Jesus said to Him, "Lord, teach us to pray..." (Luke 11:1). These disciples could have asked the Lord to teach them many things, such as how to teach, heal, raise the dead, and so on. Yet, the only recorded act the disciples ever asked Jesus to teach them was to pray. These disciples did not ask Jesus to teach them *how* to pray, but just to *pray*. It is possible to know how to pray and still not do it.

Every Christian should make this same request. No believer should play "hooky" from the school of prayer. For a Christian, learning to pray is not optional; it is essential. Martin Luther once said, "To be a Christian without prayer is no more possible than to be alive without breathing."

Many Christians live in habitual defeat when it comes to enjoying a consistent prayer life. Most believers know more about prayer than they have personally experienced. Developing a regular and meaningful life of prayer is not easy. Harold Lindsell declares, "Prayer doesn't come naturally to man. Learning to pray ... includes knowledge of the laws governing prayer as well as experience gained in the practice of prayer."[2] Let's enroll in Christ's school of prayer and with humble, hungry hearts request of Him, "Lord, teach us to pray..."

In my journey with Christ, I struggled with the discipline of prayer for many years. The other disciplines, such as Bible study, giving, etc. were fairly solid, but enjoying a consistent and meaningful conversation with God was missing. So, I understand the struggle. This book is for you. It is for any believer who desires to enjoy a better personal prayer life. It is biblical, so practical, and easy to follow.

This book is divided into three parts:

Part One (Chapters 1-2) covers Prayer Basics.

Part Two (Chapters 3-6) presents an old but practical and useful plan for praying: the ACTS acronym. You'll find it helpful.

Part Three (Chapters 7-11) examines some key issues related to enjoying a meaningful and powerful life in prayer.

PART ONE
PRAYER BASICS

Chapter 1

WHAT IS "PRAYER"?

J ust what is this business of prayer, anyway? No human has all the answers to prayer. Any teaching on the subject of prayer should begin with some basic definitions of prayer. How can prayer best be defined? We should first realize that prayer should be more than just words. **Real prayer involves all of life** (Phil. 4:6). Many times, we hear people speak about the secular and the sacred parts of life. For a Christian, no such separation should exist. Every day is to be a "holy" day for a Christian, and everything a child of God does should be seen as "spiritual," i.e., in effect, an *attitude of prayer*. Prayer is so much more than words; it is a lifestyle of worship. Since prayer touches every aspect of the Christian life, it can be described in various ways.

How does the Bible define "prayer"? In the Bible, there are twelve Hebrew words and five Greek words translated into the English word "prayer," each with the primary meaning of talking to God.

Prayer is basically conversation with God. I like Barry Wood's definition: "Prayer is conversation between an ordinary human being and an extraordinary God, often about very ordinary things."[1] God primarily converses with us when we read and study the Bible, God's love letter to us. In prayer, we converse with Him.

Chapter 2

WHY PRAY AT ALL?

I n the previous chapter, we examined some biblical definitions of prayer. We will now look into the purposes of prayer. God made us in such a way that we usually need to know the purpose and benefit of something to be motivated to do it. In reality, prayer can be best defined by what prayer *does*. As we come to better understand what prayer accomplishes, we will better understand what prayer is. To pray as Scripture requires, we must first desire to pray. How is a desire to pray developed? We must see the present and future benefits of prayer. Here are several reasons or purposes for prayer:

I. To KNOW and WORSHIP GOD

Prayer always begins with God, not us. In essence, prayer is worship. As we pray, we are recognizing the presence and worth of God. God deserves our worship. He wants us to know Him intimately (Ps. 46:10;

John 4:20-24; 17:3; Phil. 3:10). In order to know God, we must communicate with Him and He with us. How does God communicate with us? He **communicates with us** through various means:[1] (1) through Jesus in the context of Scripture; (2) through the Body of Christ, the Church; (3) through other individuals; (4) through nature; (5) through the Holy Spirit; and (6) through our minds. **We commune with God in prayer.** As I have stated before, prayer is simply conversation with God. It is dialogue between God and man in which we come to know Him better. E. M. Bounds said, "He knows not God who knows not how to pray."[2] In prayer, we come to recognize and worship God for His character and attributes—His power, majesty, faithfulness, love, holiness, forgiveness, wisdom, patience, etc. God seeks our worship (John 4:20-24), and the best way to worship Him is in prayer. A. R. Gesswein said, "There are many churchgoers, but few worshipers, because there are few 'pray-ers.'"[3]

II. To OBEY GOD

God demands that His children pray. Through the prophet Jeremiah, God said, "Call to me and I will answer you..." (Jer. 33:3). This is not an option; it is a command. He calls us to prayer, and when we do not heed the call of God, we disobey the command of God. As sovereign King, He never suggests; He commands. Though we may not fully understand why God commands us to pray, that is no excuse for disobedience. The issue is **not why** God wants us to pray **but that** He wants us to pray

(Matt. 6:5-9; 7:7-8; Luke 18:1; Phil. 4:6; 1 Thess. 5:17). It is a matter of obedience.

III. To RELEASE the POWER of GOD

There is a dynamic about prayer. Prayer works as it releases the unlimited power of our omnipotent God. **Prayer can do anything that God can do—and He can do anything!** Our prayers, in concert with the will of God, send God into action. When we pray aright, God goes to work. James said, "The prayer of a righteous man has great power as it is working" (James 5:16b).

The seminar notebook from "Change the World School of Prayer" lists several ways that **prayer releases its power**:[4]

- In prayer, there is power **for sharing God's Word**. E. W. Kenyon said, "Church history proves that the ministry of prayer makes the ministry of the Word a powerful thing."

- In prayer, there is power **for lasting revival**. R. A. Torrey, who witnessed many revivals, wrote, "There have been revivals without much preaching; but there has never been a mighty revival without mighty praying."

- The power of prayer **touches others**. Prayer does more than affect the one who prays. Prayer power also reaches out to God on behalf of others. O. Hallesby writes, "Whenever we touch His almighty arm, some of His omnipotence streams in upon us, into our souls and into our bodies. And not only that, but, through us, it streams out to others. This power is so rich and so mobile that all we have to do when we pray is to point to the persons or things to which we desire to have this power applied, and He, the Lord of this power, will direct the necessary power to the desired place at once."

People are saved and lives are touched because somebody prayed.

IV. To GLORIFY GOD

Every aspect of the Christian life is first for God's glory, and then for man's benefit (John 14:13). Everything about prayer, then, should seek to glorify God, lift up His name, and exalt His holiness. The reason we pray, and the reason God answers, is so that He can display His glory. The glory of God must be the chief aim and the very soul and life of our every prayer. There is no one glorious but the Lord. Creation exists to show His glory. All that is not for His glory is sin. Prayer brings proper glory to God (John 15:7-8; Matt. 6:13).

V. To ENFORCE CHRIST'S VICTORY OVER SATAN

Prayer blesses God and bothers Satan. Satan and his demons are the enemies of prayer. He is a thief come to steal, kill, destroy, and devour (John 10:10; 1 Pet. 5:8)! Samuel Chadwick said, "The one concern of the devil is to keep the saints from prayer. He fears nothing from prayerless studies, prayerless work, and prayerless religion. He laughs at our toil, mocks at our wisdom, but trembles when we pray."[5] Satan is not concerned about church rituals, but he is deathly fearful of genuine prayer.

A main reason to pray is to overcome Satan, the archenemy of God. As we learn warfare praying, we see Christ's authority enforced over Satan and demons. No wonder Satan fears the power of prayer more than anything. He adamantly opposes the prayer of God's people (Dan. 10:10-21). Andrew Murray said, "God's children can conquer everything by prayer. Is it any wonder that Satan does his utmost to snatch that weapon from Christians or to hinder them in the use of it?"[6] As we learn to pray with authority, we are able to hinder the power of the enemy and watch his forces submit to the will of God. The only hope Satan has is to stop our praying.

VI. To UNDERSTAND the PURPOSES and PLAN of GOD

Whenever we know the Word of God and pray in concert with the will of God, we are aligning our lives with the purpose and plan of God (1 John 5:14-15). Prayer then becomes the thrilling experience of finding God's will and praying for it (Matt. 6:10). David Hubbard explains, "Prayer reminds us of our constant need for God and reassures us of His presence with us. Prayer is part of God's plan for our growth and for His program in the world. In prayer we don't tell God what to do; we find out what He wants us to do."[7] Therefore, genuine prayer is not your effort to move God; rather, you and God are partners in bringing His will to pass through prayer.

VII. To FOLLOW the BIBLICAL EXAMPLES

Abraham, Moses, Elijah, Daniel, Jesus, Paul, and many others were people of prayer. Our Lord instructed His disciples to pray, and He modeled prayer in His life. Praying was a natural part of His life. In the four gospel records, there are not less than fifteen recorded occasions in which He prayed. Here's a capsule of His life of prayer:[8]

- His ministry **commenced with** and **counted upon** prayer (Luke 3:21; 5:15-16).

- His men were **chosen in** prayer (Luke 6:12-13).

- His miracles were **consummated by** prayer (Mark 6:41; John 11:41-42).

- His **earthly ministry concluded in** prayer (Matt. 26:36; Luke 23:46).

- His **heavenly ministry continues in** prayer (Heb. 4:14-16; 7:17, 24, 25).

E. M. Bounds declared, "Prayer was the secret of His power, the law of His life, the inspiration of His toil, and the source of His wealth, His joy, His communion and strength. To Christ Jesus prayer occupied no secondary place, but was exacting and paramount, a necessity, a life, the satisfying of a restless yearning, and a preparation for heavy responsibilities."[9]

VIII. To PLEASE GOD

Jesus's life was directed at pleasing the Father. He stated, "I always do what is pleasing to Him" (John 8:29). Paul reinforced this aim in 2 Corinthians 5:9, when he said, "So whether at home or away, we make it our aim to please Him." One thing that brings pleasure to our heavenly Father is His children praying. The writer of Proverbs said, "the prayer of the upright is acceptable to him" (Prov. 15:8b).

God not only demands that we pray, He desires and is pleased when we pray. In fact, God Himself is the initiator of prayer! As stated before, **prayer begins with God** and not with us. We tend to see prayer as something *we do*, rather than something *we join*. God is pleased with our fellowship. He desires our drawing near (James 4:8; Heb. 10:19-22).

IX. To CHANGE OURSELVES

Many wonder, "**Why pray at all**? Does it really change anything? Can my prayers change the mind of God? The Bible tells us that God does not change (James 1:17). His mind does not change. Things may change and often do, but God does not change.

Prayer changes me first and most. Prayer feeds my soul. As we pray to a holy Father, we become keenly aware of our own unholiness. Such awareness should bring confession and assurance of forgiveness. When our prayers are consistent with His will, God provides our requests (James 4:2; Matt. 6:11; 7:7). Our Father has unlimited gifts and promises for His children (Luke 11:11-13). Prayer is not so much getting what we want as it is asking God to give us what He wants. This is the key that unlocks God's promise-house. Richard Trench declared, "Prayer is not overcoming God's reluctance; it is laying hold of God's willingness."[10]

No child of God will ever effectively live for Christ and efficiently serve the cause of Christ as long as his prayer life is defective and inadequate.

CONCLUSION: Why pray? The purposes of prayer demand that prayer be given priority. Prayer is the very breath of spiritual life. Prayerlessness is not a weakness; it is a sin. It is a sin against the:

> Person and glory of God – He deserves our worship
> and demands our obedience.
> Power of God – He works for us and against Satan
> when we pray.
> Purposes of God – His plans are enacted as we pray.
> Pleasure of God – He delights in our praying.

An unknown Christian said, "The secret of all failure is our failure of secret prayer."[11]

PART TWO
A-C-T-S

Chapter 3

LET'S BEGIN WITH ADORATION

To execute anything well, you need a plan or a strategy. Praying, having a conversation with God, is no different. Though not original with me, I have found using the acronym ACTS helps create a balance in my prayer life. A is for Adoration and praise. C is for Confession. T is for Thanksgiving. S is for Supplication, praying for others and for yourself. Let's look at each.

The Church of Jesus Christ has been robbed of one of its most valuable treasures: praise. In Psalm 150:6, David stated, "Let *everything* that has breath praise the Lord." Praying includes praising, yet praise is much more than one facet of prayer. Praise should be a way of life. Psalm 119:164 says, "Seven times a day I praise you for your righteous rules." Let us learn together a lifestyle of praise.

I. WHAT IS "PRAISE"?

Praise is simply **adoration and worship of God for who and all He is.** We *adore* God as we acknowledge Him and speak to Him. To *worship* is to ascribe "worth-ship" to God. It is to give Him the glory and honor that is rightfully due Him. To adore and worship God is to pronounce that He alone is worthy of honor and glory—that is, praise (2 Sam. 22:4; Ps. 18:3). The full meaning of praise is discovered in its Old French origin, "preiser," which means "to prize." To praise God is to prize God![1]

The premier word for praise in the Bible is "hallelujah." This is a combination of two words. The first, "hallal," means "to boast, to brag on, to laud, to make a show, even to the point of looking foolish." The second, "jah," is only a shorter name for God! Hallelujah is found twenty-four times in the Old Testament, all between Psalm 104 and 150. All the hallelujahs in the New Testament are found in Revelation 19—only four times. Joining the two words "hallal" and "jah," all that is needed to make "hallelujah" complete is "u"![2]

II. WHY PRAISE AT ALL?

The supreme motivation behind praise is found in the psalmist's words in 50:23: "Whoever offers praise glorifies me." **Praise glorifies God**. God's glory is all He is—His character, His works, and His benefits. We are commanded to praise the name of the Lord in Psalm 113:3: "From the rising of the sun to its setting, the name of the Lord is to be praised." Psalm 115:1 further says, "Not to us, O Lord, not to us, but to Your name give glory..." God's name stands for who and all He is. His names are an extension of His character. There are many other psalms which speak to praising His name (Ps. 8:1; 29:1; 30:4; 34:4; 48:10; 61:8; 66:4; 72:18; 99:3; 100:4; 103:1b; 145:2).

Some common names for God used in the Old Testament:

- *ELOHIM* is used over 2,700 times in the Bible. It is found thirty-two times in Genesis 1. It means "one who is great, mighty, and dreadful."
- *EL SHADDAI* is found forty-eight times in the Old Testament. It means "God Almighty." God is mighty enough to completely nourish, satisfy, and sustain us. He is the all-sufficient God.
- *ADONAI* is used some 300 times in the Old Testament. This name refers to God's ownership and rulership of everything that is. This name suggests Lordship on His part and stewardship and submission on our part.
- *YAHWEH* is the most used name for God in the Bible, occurring over 6,800 times! It is derived from the verb "to be." He is the great "I AM" (Ex. 3:14). He is the One who is. He is self-existent and self-sufficient.

Ancient Hebrew did not use vowels in its written form. The vowels were pronounced in spoken Hebrew but not recorded in written

Hebrew. The appropriate sounds of Hebrew words were passed down orally. Thus, YHWH, also known as the tetragrammaton, is the most common written name of God in the Old Testament. There is discussion among scholars concerning which vowels should be inserted. As the Bible was translated into Latin and then German, YHWH was pronounced "Jehovah." To the Jews, God's name was so sacred that they refused to say it, so when they came to YHWH in the Old Testament, they would say "Lord (Adonai)." In keeping with this tradition, most English translations put LORD (all caps) as the translation for YHWH.

Many other names in the Old Testament are associated with Yahweh/Jehovah. Each reveals some aspect of His character and some aspect of our need.

- Jehovah – *Jireh* (Gen. 22:14) – "The Lord provides"
- Jehovah – *Rophe* (Ex. 15:26) – "The Lord heals"
- Jehovah – *Nissi* (Ex. 17:15) – "The Lord our Banner"
- Jehovah – *M'Kaddesh* (Lev. 20:7) – "The Lord who sanctifies"
- Jehovah – *Shalom* (Judges 6:24) – "The Lord our Peace"
- Jehovah – *Rohi* (Ps. 23:1) – "The Lord my Shepherd"
- Jehovah – *Tsidkenu* (Jer. 23:5-6) "The Lord our Righteousness"
- Jehovah – *Shammah* (Ezek. 48:35) – "The Lord is present"
- *JESUS* is all these. Jesus is a form of the Hebrew names Joshua, Jeshua, or Jehoshua, the basic meaning of which is "Jehovah (Yahweh) will save." Our Lord Jesus is the full revelation of God.

All that God is can be found in His name. He is in Christ, and He is all that Christ is, in me (Col. 1:27; 2:9-10).

Praise glorifies God for all He is and does. The reasons for and possibilities of praise are beyond the finite human mind. Since God is infinite, our praise should also be infinite.

III. WHY PRAISE FIRST?

Praise is the most appropriate way to begin prayer. Adoration and worship both imply we acknowledge God as God. Harold Lindsell says, "Since adoration brings man into immediate and direct contact with God, in the role of servant to Master, or the created to the Creator, it is foundational to all other kinds of prayer."[3]

Praise, alongside thanksgiving, is the **only access** into the presence of God. The psalmist writes, "Enter his gates with thanksgiving and his courts with praise" (Ps. 100:4). **Praise is where God lives.** He is at home in praise. Psalm 22:3 reads, in the King James, "But thou art holy, O thou inhabitest the praises of Israel."

Everything God made, He made to praise Him. The psalmist says, "Let everything that has breath praise the Lord" (Ps. 150:6). Praise is obligatory upon:

- Angels (Ps. 103:20; 148:2; Isa. 6:3; Rev. 4:9-11; 5:12)

- Creation (Ps. 148:1-10; 150:6)
- All men (Isa. 43:21; Ps. 107:8; 145:21)
- Saints (Eph. 1:13-14; Ps. 30:40; 149:5)
- Children (Ps. 8:2; with Matt. 21:16)
- High and low (Ps. 148:1, 11)
- Young and old (Ps. 148:1,12)
- Small and great (Rev. 19:5)

Praise is the reason for the existence of the universe, mankind, and all creation. Praise is primary! If mankind refuses to do what it was created to do, then even "the stones will cry out!" (Luke 19:37-40).

Another reason praise is first is that Jesus taught us in the model prayer (Matt. 6:9-13) to begin with adoration. He said, "Hallowed be Thy name" (Matt. 6:9). To be hallowed is to be set apart. To begin prayer in a season of praise is to set God apart as the object of our worship, positioning God in His rightful place at the very outset of our praying. Praise shifts our focus from self to God.

IV. SOME WAYS TO PRAISE OUR GOD

Jack Taylor suggests praise is adoration of God that is vocal, audible, or visible.[4] Praise can be any or all of these. Praise can be **vocal** (Ps. 145:21; 63:3; 66:1; 26:7), it may be **audible** (Ps. 47:1a; 150:3-5), and it can also be **visible** (Ps. 63:4; 149:3; 1 Chron. 15:28-29).

Though the desire to praise is present in every true believer, we need to learn how to praise at certain times and as a way of life. Here are some suggested ways:

- Study praise, worship, and adoration in God's Word.
- Memorize Scripture, especially praise portions (Ps. 56:10).
- Learn to use hymns, choruses, and other songs (Ex. 15; Judg. 5:3; Ps. 7:17; 9:11; 28:7; 47:6-7; 119:172; etc.).
- Play instruments in a way that praises (1 Chron. 16:41-42; Ps. 33:2-3; 150:3, 5).

V. WHAT RESULTS WHEN GOD'S PEOPLE PRAISE?

Praise produces powerful effects. Something happens when God's people praise.

- **We gain greater knowledge of and access to God** (Ps. 100:4; 22:3). Praise is like a straight line; it is the shortest distance between God and me (Deut. 33:1-7).
- **Praise wins over worry and depression** (Isa. 61:1-3). Worry will inevitably lead to the despair of depression, and nothing cures depression like a good dose of praise. The continual wearing of the "garment of praise" will win over discouragement, despair, and depression.
- **God is glorified** when we praise (Ps. 50:23).

- **Satan and his demons flee** from praise (Ps. 8:2; 149:4-9; Matt. 21:16). Praise is one of a Christian's most powerful weapons against the enemy. There is a mysterious power in praise that stops the devil dead in his tracks.

- **Praise results in the earth producing more** (Ps. 67:5-7). Praise is a law written into the very framework of the universe (Eph. 1:13-14; Isa. 43:21; Ps. 148). Since praise is God's law, then praise releases the power of God to do His work of productivity.

- **Praise results in generous giving** (Prov. 3:9; 1 Chron. 29:1-25; 2 Cor. 9:11-15). It is possible to give and not praise, but praise cannot exist without giving. Learning to praise is learning to give.

- **Miracles and victory can be wrought through praise** (2 Chron. 20; John 2:9; Acts 16:25; Judg. 1:1, 19-20; Josh. 14:6-12). Jack Taylor writes, "People who praise best reflect their reigning Lord. The history of praise is the history of God's mighty hand at work in the lives of mankind. Victory has always accompanied praise. It always will..."[5]

- **The sacrifice of praise improves personal worship, which enhances corporate worship**. People who praise the Lord are best prepared for and are more able to add to public worship (Psa. 9:14; 100:4; 118:19-20; Heb. 2:12).

- **Those who praise enjoy the success of God's blessings** (Luke 6:38a; Deut. 33:1-7). People who bless God by praise are blessed by God in return (Isa. 58:14).

- **Praise leaves no room for pride.** Pride is destroyed by praise (2 Chron. 26)!

Praise works. Like prayer, praise is powerful in its effects! "Through Him then let us continually offer up a sacrifice of praise to God, that is, the fruit of lips that acknowledge His name" (Heb. 13:15, RSV).

CONCLUSION: God is forever, and so it is with praise. Praise is eternal; it has always been so. God is "ever being praised" (Rom. 1:25; Psa. 61:8; 72:19; 111:10b). When we see God for who He is, we will praise Him as we ought! We need to practice praise. Develop a praise-life. Pray for the ability to praise (Psa. 51:15; 119:175). The more we praise, the more natural it becomes. Things (and people) go better with praise—so:

PRAISE THE LORD!

HALLELUJAH!!

AMEN!!!

Chapter 4

CONTINUE IN CONFESSION

I n the last chapter, we learned that praise is the doorway into the presence of God. The psalmist told us to "enter...His courts with praise" (Ps. 100:4). We need to remember that we only have access to God because of His grace and mercy supremely revealed in the person and finished work of Jesus Christ, His Son (Dan. 9:16; Lam. 3:22; Rom. 5:2; 2 Cor. 5:21; Heb. 10:19-20).

Upon entering the presence of an absolutely holy God in true prayer, I become acutely aware of my sinfulness and my need for forgiveness (Isa. 6:1-5; Job 42:1-6; Luke 5:8). Having begun in praise, how do I continue in confession?

I. WHAT IS "CONFESSION"?

As we understand the meaning of confession, we come to see its important role in the believer's prayer life. In the Old Testament, the verb "confess" and the noun "confession" both refer to the open acknowledgment of sin, whether by one individual or by the community.[1] Such confession of sin always brought God's full forgiveness (Ps. 32:5; Prov. 28:13).

Confession in the New Testament has virtually the same meaning. The word for confession of sins in the New Testament is "homologeo, "the combination of two Greek words, "homos," meaning "the same," and "lego," which means "to speak." [2] Combining these, confession means "to speak the same thing as another" or "to agree with another." *Confession in the Bible is simply agreeing with God that your sin is your sin.*

To confess is to say the same thing about sin that God says about it. This includes agreeing with God as to all the implications of sin as it relates to the Christian who commits it, and to our holy God against whom it is committed. This further entails the Christian's hatred of the sin, his sense of guilt because of it, his contrition because of it, and his determination to put it out of his life and never do it again.[2] In the New Testament, "homologeo" is used only five times (Matt. 3:6; Mk. 1:5; Acts 19:18; Jam. 5:16; 1 Jn. 1:9). As was true in the Old Testament, a person who confesses is promised God's forgiveness.

II. THE ELEMENTS OF CONFESSION

True biblical confession touches all of the Christian's life. When a believer truly confesses his sins to God, his mind, emotions, and will are all changed in some fashion. As I understand confession, it includes several elements:

- **Admittance** of the sin committed against God. This affects our mind as we acknowledge our disobedience. Before we ever willingly turn from our sin in repentance, we must first admit that what we did or did not do is sin (Ps. 32:5; 51:4). But confession is not just admitting that we sinned; it is saying that we did it against God.

- **Brokenness** over the sin. This affects our emotions as we are sorry for our sin (2 Cor. 7:8-10). Contrition, or penitence, always accompanies true confession (Luke 15:19), but true confession goes beyond admitting our sin and feeling sorry for it. Brokenness leads to changes in behavior.

- **Repentance** from disobedience to obedience. This affects our will as we change our attitude or action to conform to holiness by surrendering our will to God's (2 Cor. 5:17; 7:1; 8-11). We have not really confessed our sins until we have stopped committing them.

- **Restitution** should be made wherever it is necessary.

- **Accepting** God's forgiveness.

III. WHAT DO CHRISTIANS CONFESS?

It should go without saying that a Christian should be daily confessing his sins—but which sins? What sins? The answer? All sins! All sin is an affront to God's grace and holiness. **God hates all sin**. Every sin ever committed is basically and ultimately against God (Ps. 51:4).

Unconfessed sin in the life of a believer is the greatest hindrance to praying effectively (Ps. 66:18; Prov. 15:29; Isa. 1:13-15; 59:1-2). We should confess to God every sin of commission, omission, or neglect, spoken words, evil thoughts, and so on. **No sin is too small to hinder prayer**. It doesn't make sense to pray for anything when there is unconfessed sin in the believer's life. In fact, the wise writer of Proverbs says, "He who conceals his sins does not prosper, but whoever confesses and renounces them finds mercy" (Prov. 28:13).

Praying when we are walking in disobedience is powerless praying. Right living has always been an essential condition for proper prayer (James 5:16). Lehman Strauss writes, "No one can both sin and pray. True prayer will prevent us from sinning, or sin will prevent us from praying."[3]

IV. THE PATTERN OF CONFESSION

You may ask, "Just *how* am I to confess my sins to the Father? Is there some pattern that is helpful as I continue my prayer in confession?" We should confess:

- **Daily** – The flow of 1 John 1:9 implies continual confession of sins. Continual confessing of sins should characterize every believer's life.

- **Specifically** – We commit our sins specifically and not generally. We should take our sins serious enough to deal with them in a definite and specific manner. Let God's Spirit search your heart for sins (Ps. 139:23-24), then specifically confess each sin to the Lord.

"Does God grow weary of repeated confessions of the same sins?" If God were like men, we would think He would get sick and tired of hearing the same thing over and over again. But our God is not that way! He delights in mercy. Mercy is an act of His character that gives Him glory. God loves to forgive, and He'll forgive as often as we come to Him (Neh. 9:17; Mic. 7:18; Rom. 5:20). If we know God has forgiven all our sins, and that no matter how many times we come back and ask His forgiveness, He's eager to do it, then such love should discourage our sinning and compel us to obey rather than to sin.

- **Responsibly** – Sins committed should be handled responsibly. Right the wrong you have done as much as you can.

- **Thankfully** – Thank God for His complete forgiveness (1 John 1:9; Psa. 103:10a-12; 130:3-4; Mic. 7:18; Isa. 38:17; 43:25; Job 11:6; Ezra 9:13).

- **Confidently** – Leave your time of confession confidently believing that if you genuinely confessed, then God—as He promises—will always graciously forgive.

"How do I distinguish between the conviction of the Holy Spirit and the accusation and condemnation of the enemy?" Satan loves to accuse Christians before God day and night (Rev. 12:10). Accusation is his secret weapon in creating feelings of guilt in the life of every believer. Such feelings of guilt will take the very heart out of Christian commitment and service. Do these feelings of guilt stem from sin? No. Guilt does not always imply sin. Guilt that is **felt** is not necessarily **true** guilt. Satan uses false guilt to make us feel guilty when there is no reason for it.

What is the enemy trying to do when he accuses us? He is attempting to remove the joy of our fellowship with the Father. When the Spirit, on the other hand, convicts us, He is trying to restore the joy of that same fellowship. It should be noted that sometimes the accuser tells the truth about our sins. Now, if the Holy Spirit is trying to restore the joy of our fellowship with God, it follows that when we confess our sins, conviction will go away, and the joy of fellowship resumes. If the joy does not return upon confession, your feelings of guilt are from satanic accusation. Scripture says, "Satan is the accuser of our brethren" (Rev. 12:10).

In summary, what is the pattern for true confession? We are to confess **daily, specifically, responsibly, thankfully, and confidently**—and God will gladly and fully forgive.

V. THE RESULTS OF CONFESSION

What happens when a believer confesses his sins? The blessings from confession far outweigh the costs of confession. These blessings include the following:

- **God is glorified** when we confess our sins (Josh. 7:1-21). Confession of sin glorifies God. Whenever we excuse our sin, we are, in effect, blaming God. We are saying we were helpless and that God allowed this mess. In doing this, we are making God responsible for sin. Whenever we try to evade our personal responsibility for sin, we are defaming the holiness of God. In confessing our sin, we are agreeing with God that our sin is ours. This glorifies God.

- As sins are confessed, cleansed, and forgiven, **the believer's joy is restored** (Ps. 51:12). Unconfessed sin saddens the heart. Though sin in a Christian's life does not forfeit salvation, it will cause the joy of it to be lost. David confessed that he had not lost his salvation, but only the full joy of it.

- **God forgives us** when we confess our sin (1 John 1:9). A Christian is continually confessing his sins and continually being cleansed and forgiven for them. When God forgives them, He also forgets them (Jer. 31:33-34; cf. Heb. 8:12; 10:17). Remember this—God and others can forgive you, but oftentimes, the effects of sins remain. Sin often leaves painful consequences.

- **Divine discipline is prevented** when a believer confesses sins. God is too holy and loving to overlook sin. Because we are His children and He loves us, He must discipline our sins—for His glory and our good (Heb. 12:5-11).

- Confession of sins **minimizes self-condemnation**. The guilt of sin brings great personal misery, but God never condemns His children (Rom. 8:1). Confessing our sin frees our conscience of faith-killing guilt. When we know God forgives us fully, then we have no right not to forgive ourselves. To fail to do so is to place ourselves over God (1 John 3:19-22). Harold Lindsell said, "Just as the surgeon lances a boil to permit the infection to drain and to heal from the inside, so confession opens the sore, drains the poison, and heals from within."[4]

- The confessing of sin helps **eliminate improper selfish requests**. Confession reminds us that we deserve nothing. It helps eliminate certain things on our checklist. A broken and contrite heart rarely demands anything (Isa. 66:2; James 4:2-3).

- Our life and service as believers becomes **more usable and effective for God** when we are confessing our sins. Confession of sin is essential for spiritual growth and productivity. God makes better use of a clean vessel. Only after Isaiah cried in confession did God send him into service (Isa. 6:5-9). Only after we are broken over our sin will we really hunger and thirst for righteousness (Matt. 5:3-6; Ps. 51:10, 13).

- Confession creates a **thankful and forgiving attitude**. Since God has forgiven us a debt we could never repay, we should be more forgiving toward others (Matt. 18:23-35; cf. Eph. 4:32). God's gracious mercy on our behalf should generate a thankful heart for all He has done for us.

CONCLUSION: Genuine confession is essential to confident praying.

Chapter 5

TRY THANKSGIVING

I'm convinced that the greatest singular act of personal worship that you can render to God is to have a thankful heart. Thanks ultimately crucifies self; thanks ultimately recognizes God as the source of everything; thanks is always able to say in the midst of difficult circumstances, "God be praised," and see beyond the pain to the plan of God (Rom. 8:28). And thanks is the ultimate act of praise because it says, "God I thank you even for the hard times, for those that die, for a difficult marriage, for an unfulfilling job. . . for everything, because I know that it can be used for my good in confirming me to Jesus Christ."[1]

Thanksgiving constitutes a very essential part of prayer. Prayer and thanksgiving are inseparably linked in the Bible (Neh. 11:17;

Phil. 4:6; Col. 4:2). Together they form a blessed combination. The psalmist said, "It is good to give thanks to the Lord…" (Ps. 92:1). A thankful spirit is a good thing to possess. Appreciation is a foundational element of healthy human relationships, and it is all the more important in our relationship with God.

Even though thanksgiving is closely related to praise (Ps. 92:1; 100:4; Heb. 13:15), it deserves to stand by itself in a season of prayer. How are praise and thanksgiving different? In praise, God is worshipped for who He is; His attributes and character are the focus of praise. In contrast, thanksgiving worships God for what He has done. His activities and conduct are the reason for our thanks. O. Hallesby writes, "When we give thanks we give God the glory for what He has done for us, and when we worship or give praise, we give God glory for who He is in Himself."[2] When we thank God, we are gratefully acknowledging His benefits and blessings in our life and in the lives of others. If we'll **think** of God's blessings, we'll **thank** Him for them. In fact, the words **think** and **thank** are derived from the same Old English root word. I'm sure if we would take time to think more, we would no doubt thank more.

Why is there thanksgiving after confession? Simply this: if confession cleanses us of our sins, then thanksgiving is the gratitude we show for sending us such a great gift—a forgiven life should generate thankful lips.

There are several important truths to understand concerning thanksgiving in prayer.

I. THANKSGIVING – TO WHOM?

Who is to be the object of our thanksgiving? More often than we'd like to admit, we are more grateful for the blessings received than the bestower Himself. **God Himself is the object of our thanksgiving.** The Giver is far more important than the gift. He gives us what He does because of who He is. Over and over, the Bible exhorts us "to give thanks **to the Lord**" (Ps. 92:1; 100:4; 105:1; 106:1; 107:1; 111:1; 118:1; etc.). To whom then are we to offer thanks? To God the Father through our Lord Jesus Christ (Rom. 1:8; Eph. 5:20; Col. 3:17).

II. THANKSGIVING – BY WHOM?

Who is admonished to observe thanksgiving to God? The Bible pictures the angels giving thanks to God (Rev. 4:9; 7:11-12; 11:16-17). Every saint is commanded to "offer to God a sacrifice of thanksgiving" (Ps. 50:14; cp. Ps. 116:17). Both the Old and New Testament exhort the believer to give prayerful thanksgiving unto God (Ps. 95:2; 100:4; Col. 2:6-7; 3:15; 1 Thess. 5:17-18).

III. THANKSGIVING – WHAT FOR?

What purposes are accomplished when God's people thank Him?

- **God is magnified** (Ps. 69:30).
- **The Father is obeyed** (Ps. 50:14; 100:4; 105:1; etc.). Gratitude warms the heart of God. Ingratitude is a heinous sin (Luke 17:11-19). Failure to say thanks is characteristic of the unsaved (Rom. 1:21). Lehman Strauss writes, "It is a rude imposition to come to God asking for anything without saying thanks for past blessings. There should be that same urgency and definitiveness in giving thanks to God as there is in asking of Him. It must be a grief to God to listen to requests from His ungrateful children."[3]
- **The believer is reminded that God is the giver of all we are and have** (James 1:17). Thanksgiving reminds us of our need for and dependence upon God. It is one thing to receive a blessing, but it's something else to be thankful for it.
- **Scripture is full of examples.** The Bible is filled with men and women who were grateful to God: David (1 Chr. 29:13), Levites (2 Chr. 5:12-13; Dan. 2:33; 6:10; Jon. 2:9), Simeon (Lk. 2:28), and Anna (Lk. 2:38). Two supreme examples of thanksgiving in prayer are from the apostle Paul and the Lord Jesus Himself. *Paul* was a thankful man (Acts 28:15; Rom. 1:8; 1 Cor. 1:4; Eph. 1:15-16; 5:20; Phil. 1:3; Col. 1:3; 1 Thess. 1:2;

3:9; 5:17-18; 2 Thess. 1:3; 2:13; 2 Tim. 1:3). *Jesus* provides the supreme example of thanksgiving in prayer (Mk. 8:6; Jn. 6:11; 11:41; Matt. 11:25; cp. Lk. 10:21; Matt. 26:27; cp. Lk. 22:19).

- **Thanksgiving is evidence of being Spirit-filled** (Eph. 5:18-20).

IV. THANKSGIVING – FOR WHAT?

For what are we to be thankful? The Bible records many particular things to be grateful for:

- Food (John 6:11; Acts 27:35)
- The completion of a great undertaking (Neh. 12:31, 40)
- God's holiness (Ps. 30:4; 97:12)
- God's goodness and mercy (Ps. 106:1; 107:1; 136:1-3)
- The gift of Christ (2 Cor. 9:15)
- Christ's power and reign (Rev. 11:17)
- The effect of God's Word (1 Thess. 2:13)
- Christ's deliverance from indwelling sin (Rom. 7:23-25)
- Victory over death and grave (1 Cor. 15:57)
- Wisdom and might (Dan. 2:23)
- Triumph of the gospel (2 Cor. 2:14)
- Conversion of others (Rom. 6:17)
- Faith exhibited by others (Rom. 1:8; 2 Thess. 1:3)
- Grace bestowed on others (1 Cor. 1:4; Phil. 1:3-5; Col. 1:3-6)
- Zeal exhibited by others (2 Cor. 8:16)

- Nearness of God's presence (Ps. 75:1)
- Appointment to ministry (1 Tim. 1:12)
- Supply of bodily wants (Rom. 14:6, 7; 1 Tim. 4:3-4)
- All men (1 Tim. 2:1)
- All things (2 Cor. 9:11; Eph. 5:20)

V. THANKSGIVING – HOW?

The element of thanksgiving should be a regular part of a Christian's prayer life. Let me offer some practical tips for your time of thanksgiving.

Thank God **"for all things"** (Eph. 5:20). No benefit from God is too small to overlook (Ps. 103:2).

Thank God **specifically**. To only generally be thankful for everything may result in being thankful for nothing. We should thank God for specific evidences of His love. Thank Him for: (1) physical blessings (health, body, etc.); (2) material blessings (clothes, home, food, job, money, etc.); (3) people blessings (parents, friends, mate, pastor, etc.); (4) spiritual blessings (salvation, wisdom, Bible, forgiveness, etc.).

Thank God **continually** (Eph. 5:20; 1 Thess. 5:18). Thanksgiving is one result of being filled with the Holy Spirit. It should be a way of life. We need to develop a "thanks consciousness." We may not be thankful for everything or every situation, but we should be thankful in all things because we know that God is in control and "all things work together for good" (Rom. 8:28).

CONCLUSION: Thanksgiving is the will of God (1 Thess. 5:18). "What shall I render to the Lord for all his benefits toward me? To thee I shall offer a sacrifice of thanksgiving, and call upon the name of the Lord" (Ps. 116:12, 17). In developing an attitude of gratitude, praying something similar to the following may be beneficial:

PRAYER OF THANKSGIVING

Lord, by Your grace I have been born into Your kingdom. I acknowledge Your sovereignty and believe You are in ultimate control over my life, today and for all eternity.

I also acknowledge that You have not guaranteed my life will be free from difficulty, nor have You promised me worldly success. But by Your grace and goodness, You have promised me abundant life in this world and eternal life in the next.

Therefore, today I willfully surrender all my rights and expectations to You. I humbly ask You to enable me by Your wonderful grace to consistently respond by giving thanks in and for everything, in whatever circumstances You allow to enter my life.

Chapter 6

CONCLUDE IN SUPPLICATION

Prayer should take you from Adoration to Confession, then to Thanksgiving, and finally to Supplication. Supplication simply means "to ask." God wants you to ask Him to meet your needs and the needs of others (Phil. 4:19). Jesus tells us, "Ask and it will be given you ... how much will your Father who is in heaven give good things to those who ask Him!" (Matt. 7:7, 11). Jesus also says, "Whatsoever you ask in my Name, this I will do, that the Father may be glorified in the Son" (John 14:13). The apostle John said this: "If we ask anything according to His will He hears us... in whatever we ask, we know that we have the requests that we have asked of Him (1 John 5:14-15). For whom do we ask? We ask on behalf of others; that's *intercession*. And we ask on our own behalf; that's *petition*. Let's take a look at each of these elements of supplication.

INTERCESSION

Intercession, earnestly praying on behalf of others, is vital in prayer. Praying for others is both crucial and biblical. It is crucial for fulfilling God's will. This does not mean that God is incapable of bringing His will to pass, but that He has chosen to include us in the accomplishing of His will. When we engage in the ministry of intercession, we actually become a vital part of seeing God's plans and purposes fulfilled.

Intercession has been called "the heart of prayer." Praying for others is one of the greatest privileges and responsibilities given to a believer. It is the divine equalizer. Not every believer can preach to others, teach to others, or sing for others, but *we can all pray for others*.

In intercession, the believer is acting as an intermediary between God and man. He forgets himself and his own needs in his identification with the needs of others. Abraham's prayers for Lot and the people of Sodom (Gen. 18:23-33) and Moses's prayers for Israel (Ex. 32:1-14, 30-35) are classic examples of intercession. There are several truths the Bible teaches concerning intercessory prayer.

I. THE PLEA FOR INTERCESSION

Paul said, "First of all, then, I urge that supplications, prayers, intercessions, and thanksgivings be made for all people..." (1 Tim. 2:1). Ephesians 6:18 speaks of "making supplication for all the saints." James 5:16 says, "pray for one another..."

Samuel told the people of Israel, "far be it from me that I should sin against the Lord by ceasing to pray for you..." (1 Sam. 12:23). We sin against God when we fail to pray for others.

Jesus sets the example for intercessory prayer. As the Incarnate God on earth, He prayed for Peter in Luke 22:31-32. He also prayed for His disciples (John 17:6-19), as well as for believers of all times (John 17:20-26). Now, as the ascended Savior of men, He continues to intercede for His followers. Hebrews 7:25 states, "He always lives to make intercession for them (us)."

Likewise, Apostle Paul believed in the ministry of intercession. He continually prayed for individuals and churches (Eph. 1:15-16; 3:14-19; Phil. 1:3-5; Col. 1:3, 9-14; 1 Thess. 1:2-3; 2 Thess. 1:3, 1-12; 2 Tim. 1:3; Philem. 4-5). Clearly, the Bible commands that we pray for one another.

II. THE CONTENT OF INTERCESSION

What do we pray when we intercede for others? All too often we tend to focus our intercessions only on the material or the physical. Though Scripture never condemns this, the Bible places a much greater emphasis on praying for spiritual blessings rather than material ones. God's Word details several spiritual blessings we should pray for one another:

- **Inner Spiritual Strength** – The fullness of the Spirit is the source of inner strength (Eph. 5:18; 3:19b). Paul prayed the saints would enjoy internal spiritual strength (Col. 1:11; Eph. 3:16). Jesus prayed that Peter's faith (strength) would not fail (Luke 22:31-32).

- **Divine Power** – Human resources are insufficient to deal with life. We need divine power (Eph. 1:19-23; Col. 1:11).

- **Supernatural Wisdom** – The wisdom of man is nothing in comparison to the wisdom of God (1 Cor. 1:18-2:16). God must provide His wisdom and understanding (James. 1:5; Col. 1:9b).

- **Moral Character** (Purity) – Pray that others will live a life consistent with being called a child of God (Col. 1:10; Eph. 4:1).

- **Thankful Heart** – Intercede for others to be thankful for the goodness of God in their lives (Col. 1:12).

- **Knowledge of God** – Nothing is more crucial than knowing God intimately. The better we know Him, the more we will understand His purpose for us (Eph. 1:17b-18a) and our position in Him (Eph. 1:18b).

- **Abounding Love for Others** – Our love for each other is evidence of our relationship to Christ (John 13:34-35). We must pray that our love will abide and abound (Eph. 3:17-9a; Phil. 1:9-11; 1 Thess. 3:12-13).

- **Effective Witness** – Intercede for believers to have open doors to share the gospel of Christ (Eph. 6:18-20; Philem. 6; Matt. 9:35-38; 2 Thess. 3:1). Open doors are essential to effective evangelism (2 Cor. 2:12-13; Rev. 3:20; Acts 14:27; 2 Cor. 16:9; Col. 4:3-4).

- **Daily Sustenance** – In the Lord's Prayer, Jesus taught us to pray for the daily needs of life (Matt. 6:11).

- **Divine Deliverance** – We need to pray for protection and deliverance (2 Thess. 3:2-3).

The content of intercession is clear; the pattern is set. We are to be primarily concerned with the spiritual dimension. Instead of praying for someone to be delivered from physical ills or trials, we should pray that he would be in right relationship to God, so he can relate to the trial with a proper attitude. Do not be so shortsighted that you stop praying for physical needs, but remember that God is much more concerned about our spiritual welfare. Intercessory prayer should primarily focus on spiritual objectives.

III. THE PATTERN FOR INTERCESSION

How should we intercede for others? There are several key elements that are part of the pattern of biblical intercession.

- **Identification with the needs of others** – To effectively pray for others, we must seek to identify with their needs. Spiritually and emotionally, we must feel what they feel. Jesus again sets the example (Matt. 20:34; 9:36; 14:14; Mark 1:41; Luke. 7:13; Heb. 4:15).

- **Motivation** – Always desire God's will for others. When praying for others, we must desire their highest good, which is always the will of God. As we intercede, we must take our hands off completely and let God work any way He sees fit.

- **Participation** – If necessary, we must be willing to be part of the answer when interceding.

- **Continuation** – When we pray for others, we must be willing to persevere and continue until the answer comes (Rom. 1:9).

IV. THE PEOPLE OF INTERCESSION

Generally, it is every believer's responsibility to "pray for all the saints" (Eph. 6:18). In addition, the Bible says there are some specific people for whom we should intercede as well:

- **Those in Places of Authority** (1 Tim. 2:1-2) – Paul tells us we are to pray for kings and all those in positions of authority. For us, this would mean our president, our congress, our governor, and others—even our boss. We should pray that all who run for public office, as well as those appointed, would fear God and acknowledge Him as Lord (Pro. 29:2).

- **The Lost** (1 Tim. 2:3-6) – Paul tells us it is God's will for everyone to be saved. Paul was burdened for the salvation of the Jews (Rom. 9:2-3; 10:1). To pray for the lost is to pray in accordance with God's will (2 Pet. 3:9). Dick Eastman suggests a plan to help us intercede for the lost. We need to ask God to cause the lost to ask themselves such questions as:[1]

o   "Whom can I trust?" Pray that God will lead the lost to look for someone to trust beyond themselves.

o   "What is my purpose for living?" Pray that lost souls will search for true meaning in life.

o   "When will I really be free?" Pray that God will bring them a deep unrest and longing to know the freedom of truth.

o   "How can I cope with life and its problems?" Pray that the lost will realize life is hopeless without God's help.

o   "Where will I go when I die?" Pray that God will cause an urgency to fill the hearts of the lost concerning their eternal destination.

To intercede for the lost is to become the mediator between a lost soul and an Almighty God. What could be more needed than prayer for the salvation of a lost soul?

- **Our Enemies** – Jesus said, "Love your enemies, bless them that curse you, do good to them that hate you, and pray for them which despitefully use you and persecute you" (Matt. 5:44).
- **Laborers** – We are to pray for those whom God calls to respond and go forth to share Him with others (Matt. 9:38).

- **Church Leaders** (Heb. 13:7, 17-19a) – We should also intercede for God's servants, especially those in full-time Christian service. Paul tells us how to pray for those who have made spiritual service their life vocation (Eph. 6:18-20):
  - o Pray that *utterance* will be given—know what to preach and teach.
  - o Pray for *boldness* to speak.
  - o Pray for the message to be *clear*.

One of the greatest tragedies of the church today is that more time is given to criticizing church leadership than praying for it.

- **Those in Bondage to the Enemy** – Satan opposes God. Interceding for others is engaging in spiritual warfare (Dan. 10:10-14). Those who have been blinded by and are in bondage to the enemy need our prayers (2 Cor. 4:4). Believers have been given the necessary power and strength to overcome all the power of the enemy (Luke 10:19).
- **For the Sick and Afflicted** – We should pray for the physical well-being of others (James 5:13-18). This subject of praying for healing is one of great controversy today. The key to all prayer for healing lies in our desire for God to be glorified. Those who teach that all sickness can and should be healed have done much damage to people and to the Lord's honor. This leads people to

despair because they are not healed, and they assume it is due to sin in their lives or a lack of faith.

A balanced biblical view leads to no such problem. To believe in the power of prayer for healing (and I do), while submitting the problem and the process to the will and glory of God, leaves us in trust and peace. Paul balanced it beautifully in 2 Corinthians 12 when his own prayer for healing or deliverance was submitted to the higher purpose of God. This resulted in no deception, no destruction of faith, but only in power and praise to God.

- **For All the Saints** (Eph. 6:18) – We are responsible to pray for one another as members of the body of Christ. The "high-priestly" intercessory prayer of our Lord in John 17 provides some tips that we can make as prayer-targets for the church:
  o God's people are *set apart* (John 17:6, 9, 10, 14).
  o God's people are *secure* (John 17:14-15).
  o God's people are *sanctified* (John 17:14, 17, 20).
  o God's people have been *sent* (John 17:18-20).
  o God's people are *seen as one* (John 17:11, 20, 21, 23).

Praying for others is priority. We need to stop focusing so much on self and instead focus more on others. When I pray for someone else, someone else will pray for me, and everybody gets covered!

God seeks intercessors but seldom finds them, which is plain in His cry through Isaiah: "He saw there was no man, and wondered that there was no intercessor" (Isa. 59:16b; Ezek. 22:30). One of the greatest ministries we have to one another is to pray for one another, so be certain to include intercession in your prayer time.

PETITION

Petition is a vital aspect of prayer. It is the element of prayer in which a believer asks God for specific, personal things. Though there are many more exhortations and examples in Scripture regarding praying for others, to unselfishly ask for spiritual or material blessings for yourself is not unscriptural (1 Chron. 4:9-10). Some sincere Christians believe they should never ask God on their behalf, but only for the needs of others. This well-meaning concept shows an incorrect view of prayer. In this matter of petitioning prayer, there are several key factors we should understand.

I. THE PRIORITY OF PETITION

Even though intercession is primary, petition holds a position of priority. An understanding of the word "petition" will enable us to see the priority of petition.

This word petition means "to beg, to lack." In Scripture, this word refers to asking for one's personal needs. The picture behind the word is that of a beggar sitting at the side of the road, begging the help of the king as he passes by. It expresses helplessness to meet one's own needs and dependence on God to meet them. Petition cries, "I cannot, but God can!" When we come, God promises we will find help in our time of need (Heb. 4:16). J. I. Packer notes, "The prayer of a Christian is not an attempt to force God's hand, but a humble acknowledgment of helplessness and dependence."[2]

Scripture plainly teaches that God wants us to share our needs and concerns with Him. Jesus said, "Ask, and it shall be given to you; seek and you shall find; knock, and it shall be opened to you. For everyone who asks receives, and he who seeks finds, and to him who knocks it shall be opened" (Matt. 7:7-8). He further taught us to pray in the Lord's Prayer, "Give us this day our daily bread" (Matt. 6:11). Paul adds, "Be anxious for nothing, but in everything by prayer and supplication with thanksgiving let your requests be made known to God" (Phil. 4:6). James saw the priority of petition when he said, "You do not have because you do not ask" (James 4:2c).

God, our heavenly Father, loves for His children to come to Him in prayer, voicing our helplessness and utter dependence upon Him. We compliment God when we ask great things of Him.

II. THE PRINCIPLES FOR PETITION

Proper petition adheres to some key biblical principles. Petition should be:

- **SIMPLE** – Petition does not have to be cluttered with fancy words. The condition of our heart is far more important than the words of our lips. Be yourself and keep your request brief and simple, but not shallow. Simply let your heart cry out to God—He knows, cares, and can do something about your petitions. Nothing is small to Him.

- **SINCERE** – There is no need to try to fool God. He is well aware of our thoughts, feelings, and intentions. Sincerity, honesty, and integrity are essential qualities of petition. We should never place our wants before His will. Sincerely desire His will over yours (Matt. 26:39).

- **SPECIFIC** – Do not petition in vague generalities. This shows an absence of real desire and concern.

- **UNSELFISH** – James 4:3 tells us, "You ask and do not receive, because you ask wrongly to spend it on your passions." What about those times when you cannot tell if your motive is right? Pray and let God decide. He is always able to give you what is best even when you ask for the wrong things and with the wrong motives. Be sure to examine your motives before asking God for anything. Even in praying for ourselves, our motive ought to be that God may be glorified in our lives, not just that we get what we desire.

- **PERSISTENT** – Many believers wonder if it is okay to repeatedly petition God. Matthew 7:7-8 tells us we are to "ask," "seek," and "knock." The Greek tense of these verbs suggest continual action.

If we persistently petition, are we guilty of praying "vain repetitions?" Jesus chided the Pharisees for such praying (Matt. 6:7), yet He was speaking not just of repetition, but of vain (empty, of no real value) repetition. He was merely addressing the "worthless" praying that the Pharisees offered primarily for show.

One word of caution—we must be careful not to be demanding in our persistence. If you impatiently demand of God, He may give you what you want though it isn't best for you. The result could be "leanness to your soul" (Ps. 106:15).

Make sure your requests are biblical. Anytime we ask anything of God for others or ourselves, our requests must be consistent with His will as revealed in His Word.

An important note—our prayers should include self-involvement. God always expects us to do our part too.

III. THE PROCEDURE IN PETITION

As was true in intercession, so it is in petition: the thrust of petition should be on spiritual blessings more than material or physical ones. Here is a suggested procedure:

- Ask God for **spiritual blessings**. Ask Him to:
  - o   allow you to know Him better.
  - o   fill you with His Spirit.
  - o   help you discover your gifts and dispense them.
  - o   make you an effective witness.

- o enable you to avoid temptation to evil.
- o make you a good steward.
- o give you a good family.
- o guide you to put on the whole armor of God.

Ask God for **material blessings** (Matt. 6:11—In this verse, "bread" is anything needed for life—food, clothes, shelter, etc.). See Proverbs 30:8-9. Ask Him for:

- a healthy body.
- food.
- clothing.
- shelter.

Petition pleases God. It delights Him. A fitting verse to conclude our study of supplication in prayer (asking for others and self) is Psalm 37:4, which says, "Delight yourself in the LORD, and He will give you the desires of your heart." If we will only seek to please Him and do His will in every area of life, then He promises that the desires we have are those He gives to us. When this happens, there is no doubt He will hear and answer our every prayer because it will be His will.

CONCLUSION: Supplication is vital in our prayer life. It is where we ask God to meet our needs and the needs of others, as well as where we find His will for our lives and for others.

PART THREE
IMPORTANT PRAYER ISSUES

Chapter 7

WINNING THE WAR
THROUGH PRAYER

Spiritual warfare is real. It is neither phony nor funny. We are all engaged in a real spiritual battle. Some of the most helpful information about enjoying an abundant Christian life is found in this area. A balanced and biblical understanding of this area will: dispel ignorance about who the enemy is and how he operates, eliminate fear, exalt the person and power of God, and encourage personal holiness. Satan hates teachings concerning spiritual warfare because he hates exposure.

I. THE WAR

The **TRUTH** of spiritual warfare comes from two sources:

1. **Testimony of Scripture** validates the reality of spiritual warfare. Seven Old Testament books make references beginning in Genesis. Every New Testament writer affirms the reality of Satan and demons (ten references in all). There are over three hundred

more references to Satan and demons than to holy angels, and over one hundred references to demons in the New Testament. There are forty-eight references to Satan in the Gospels, twenty-five of which are made by Jesus. He dealt with demonized people on earth (nine of seventeen mentioned). Paul faced it and taught on it (fifteen times), and so did Dr. Luke in Acts (eleven times). This includes John, James, Jude, and the writers of Hebrews and Revelation too. The only mention of "church" in the Gospels is by Jesus, and it is stated in the context of conflict and warfare (Matt. 16:18).

2. **Human experience** also validates the reality of spiritual warfare. Just look around and see obvious ongoing conflict. Satan is no longer in the closet. Look at TV, movies, books, etc.

The **TRAITS** of spiritual warfare, what spiritual war looks like, can be seen in Ephesians 6:12, "For we do not wrestle against flesh and blood, but against the rulers, against the authorities, against the cosmic powers over this present darkness, against the spiritual forces of evil in the heavenly places." The spiritual war we engage is:

o **Supernatural** – It is spiritual and invisible, not with flesh and blood.

o **Organized** – There is a chain of command, a hierarchy according to the function and power of the demons.

o **Intense** – There is a "wrestle," which will worsen as it nears the end.

o **Personal** – This battle is against "we": every Christian is involved.

o **Continual** – Spiritual warfare is ongoing.

The **TERRITORY** is in the mind (2 Cor. 2:11; 10:3-5; 11:3; Prov. 4:20-23; 23:7; Phil 4:8).

II. THE ENEMIES – Warfare waged on three fronts

1. The **flesh within** us (temptation) (Cor. 10:13; James 1:13-18; Matt. 4:1-11; Gal. 5:15-26). See "Prayer for Fighting Temptation"[1] in Appendix A.

2. The **world around** us (John 12:31; 15:18-27; 17:15-19; Rom. 12:1-2; James 4:1-10; 1 John 2:15-17). Below is a progression of worldliness:

| Friends with James 4:4 | Polluted by James 1:27 | Conformed to Rom. 12:2 | Love for 1 John 2:15-17 | Condemned with 1 Cor. 11:32 |

3. The **spiritual forces against** us.

*   **One Satan** (1 Pet. 5:8) – We have one adversary: the fallen angel named Lucifer (Ezek. 28:11-19; Isa. 14:12-15; Rev. 12:7-9). God made Lucifer, who became Satan through rebellion. He has many names, and he has a constant adversarial relationship with every believer.

*   **Many Demons** (Rev. 12:3-4):

o   *Reality* – The Bible does not attempt to prove the existence of demons any more than it does the existence of God or good angels.

o   *Personality* – Demons are humanlike. They fell with Lucifer and are fallen angelic beings with evil minds, rebellious wills, and many emotions. All are evil, have great strength, and are restless without bodies.

III. THE WILES (2 Cor. 2:11; Eph. 6:11)

- They **discover** ground. Satan and his demons are "seeking" (1 Pet. 5:8) believers who have given them "opportunity" by unconfessed sins (Eph. 4:27).

A PRAYER TO TAKE BACK GROUND

Blessed heavenly Father, I ask Your forgiveness for offending You by committing this sin of (name the offense). I claim the cleansing that is mine through the blood of the Lord Jesus Christ. I address myself against Satan and all of his kingdom. I take away from you and all your powers of darkness any ground you are claiming against me when I sinned in (name the offense). I claim that ground back in the name of the Lord Jesus Christ. I cover it with the blood of the Lord Jesus Christ and give all areas of my life over to the full control of the Holy Spirit.

- They **deceive** minds through lies that state God cannot be believed (2 Cor. 2:11; 10:3-5; 11:3). Demons will use unbelief, ignorance, error, etc. Watch out for false teachers (2 Tim. 3:1-5).
- They **develop** strongholds (2 Cor. 10:3-5), or unholy habits of disobedience. Strongholds are demonically controlled power bases that enslave us (ex: sexual sins, wrongful anger, abnormal fears, unforgiving spirit, rebellious attitudes, immoral behavior, occult involvement, etc.) Strongholds result in a continuum of sin.

THE CONTINUUM OF SIN

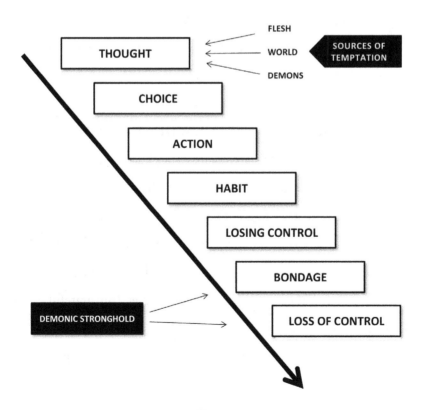

- What is Satan's Goal? To **destroy** our effectiveness as Christians. He cannot take our salvation, but if we let him, he can make our walk with Christ ineffective.

IV. THE WEAPONS (2 Cor. 10:3-5)

- Words of **praise** (Ps. 149:5-9) – The enemy hates our praise; God inhabits it.
- The **Word** of God (Matt. 4:1-11) – This is also known as the Sword of the Spirit (Eph. 6:17b).
- The **Cross** of Christ (Col. 2:13-15) – Satan disarmed and defeated.
- **Angels** of protection that guard us (Ps. 91:11; 34:7).
- The **Holy Spirit** in us that empowers us (Eph. 6:10; 1 John 4:4).
- The **whole armor** of God (Eph. 6:13-17).

A PRAYER TO PUT ON THE WHOLE ARMOR OF GOD

Dear heavenly Father, I recognize that I am engaged in a spiritual conflict with supernatural forces. I realize that this Christian life is not a playground, but a battleground. Lord, I also know that apart from You I am without wisdom and power to overcome the enemy. Lord, I'm so thankful that my position in Christ is already settled and secure—I'm already seated in the heavenlies with You. Father, I am grateful that You have already provided all the resources I need to overcome the enemy in my daily walk with You—and I take full responsibility in appropriating these resources!

Dear Lord, I thank and praise You for Your great and precious promises that tell me, "Greater is He that is in me, than he that is in the world." At the cross, Christ gave a death blow to Satan.

Today, Lord, I want to be strong in You and in the strength of Your might; I am putting on the whole armor of God, so I'll be able to stand firm and resist the enemy.

I put on the belt of *truthfulness*. I want to be ready and committed to fight the battle by having an attitude of truthfulness today.

Next, I put on the *breastplate of righteousness*. I want to be holy and pure in my life today. I need my mind and my emotions to be protected by living a godly life.

I *shod my feet with the preparation of the gospel of peace*. I am firmly planted in the truth that You are on my side.

Next, I take up the *shield of faith* with which I will be able to quench all the fiery darts of the seducing temptations of the evil one. I resolve this day to live by faith and to believe You—Your power and Your promises. I want to consistently apply what the Bible teaches about You to every situation I face today.

I also take up the *helmet of salvation*. I am thankful for the sure hope of ultimate salvation and victory in Christ.

Finally, I take up the *sword of the Spirit, which is the Word of God*. I believe the Word and know it will supply all I need today in the conflict. I pray for wisdom to apply specific scriptures to specific situations today.

Heavenly Father, thank you for all of these provisions. I love You and submit my life this day to the controlling power of Your Holy Spirit.

This is my prayer in the strong name of the Lord Jesus Christ, Amen!

- **Warfare praying** (Eph. 6:18-20). Note: Additional spiritual warfare prayers can be found in Appendix A: "Spiritual Warfare Prayers."
- The **name** of the Lord Jesus Christ (Acts 16:18). Recognize, respect and resist the enemy in the name of the Lord Jesus Christ (1 Pet. 5:8-9).

V. THE WINNERS

- The enemy was **defeated** at the cross (Col. 2:13-15; Heb. 2:14-15; 1 John 3:8)—stripped of his power.
- The ultimate **destiny** of Satan and his demons is certain eternal confinement (Matt. 25:41; Rev. 20:7-10)—the sentence has been announced; execution is awaiting!

CONCLUSION: Waking up to warfare should bring more consistent victory in your daily Christian walk. We should "be sober and alert, our enemy prowls around..." We should remember, "We are more than conquerors..." The question is not, "Do you have the victory?" but, "Are you standing in the victory you already have in Christ?" (1 Cor. 15:57; Rom. 8:37; 1 John 5:4).

Chapter 8

DOES GOD ANSWER PRAYER?

GOD ANSWERS PRAYER! A person who doubts this will probably give little time to prayer. Charles Spurgeon bluntly reminds us, "We ought not to tolerate for one minute the ghastly and grievous thought that God will not answer prayer. His nature, as manifested in Christ Jesus, demands it.[1]"

Still, many prayers utterly fail in accomplishing any results. Countless prayers go up and bring nothing down. Prayer is sometimes like dialing a phone and getting a busy signal or being put on hold, which can lead many to wonder if God does answer our prayers.

Everyone needs to talk to the Father and know **He can and does hear and answer all prayers.** God answers prayer in one of several different ways: directly, differently, with delay, and with a denial.

I. DIRECT Answers to Prayer

Sometimes God answers a specific request almost immediately and exactly as we had prayed. It is exciting to see the Father instantly respond to a request from His child. There are many *examples* of direct answers to prayer in the Scriptures: Abram's prayer for an heir (Gen. 15:2-6); Eliezer's prayer to find a wife for Isaac (Gen. 24:12-14); Elijah's prayer for the widow's son to be revived (1 Kings 17:21-22); Elisha's prayer that the son of the Shunammite couple revive (2 Kings 4:33-35); Jabez's prayer to enlarge his coasts (1 Chr. 4:10); Hezekiah's prayer to live (2 Kings 20:1-3); Jesus's prayer to raise Lazarus (John 11:41-42), and many more.

II. DIFFERENT Answers to Prayer

Oftentimes, God will answer in a way that is different than we desire. Our sinfulness and shortsightedness sometimes cause us to pray wrongly. For instance, Paul thought he needed healing, but God knew Paul needed grace (2 Cor. 12:7-9). God's ways and wisdom are so much higher and better than ours. In His love, He will sometimes answer prayer in a different manner than we desire—Father knows best! Other examples of God answering prayer differently than expected are in Genesis 17:18; Numbers 12:13; 21:7-9; and John 6:34-35.

III. DELAYED Answers to Prayer

When we feel we have unselfishly prayed and in the will of God, we should not be discouraged as we wait. Sometimes God delays the answer, and we usually interpret this as a "no." Our schedule of reply does not always match His. A request deferred is not always a request denied. **God's delays are not necessarily His denials.** Moses prayed and asked God to permit him to enter the Promised Land, but the answer was delayed fifteen hundred years! Moses did not arrive until Jesus brought him there on the Mount of Transfiguration (Matt. 17:1-8).

There are usually two basic reasons why we must wait. One is God's sovereignty. God knows not only what is best, but also when it is best. Let God work in His own perfect time. God's clock is never slow; He is always on time. God may say **"wait"** because we are not yet ready to receive what we desire, or He may delay His answer so that greater glory may come to Himself. Sometimes, then, the delay is intentional on God's part.

Secondly, Satan's intervention sometimes delays the answer. God may have answered a prayer immediately, only to have the answer delayed in transmission. Satan has the power to hold the answer back—for a while—to delay the result—for a time. This was the experience of the prophet Daniel as he recorded it in Daniel 10:12-13. From Daniel's experience, we see the warfare that exists between the forces of heaven and hell when a Christian prays.

When you sense warfare in your praying, exercise your God-given authority by putting on the whole armor of God for protection, and praying in the name of the Lord Jesus Christ, through His shed blood, which represents Satan's defeat (Luke 10:17-20; Eph. 6:10-20; Prov. 18:10; Rev. 12:11).

Does the Bible record any examples of delayed or qualified answers to prayer? There are four striking examples to consider: Moses's request to enter Canaan (Deut. 3:23-29), Hannah's prayer for a son (1 Sam. 1:1-20), Paul's thorn (2 Cor. 12:7-10), **and** Jesus's prayer in Gethsemane (Matt. 26:36-46).

IV. DENIED Request in Prayer

Sometimes God denies giving us our prayer request. Most believers do not understand or appreciate this response. When God says "no," that is an answer. Moses, Elijah, and Job all prayed to die, and God denied their request (Num. 11:11-15; 1 Kings 19:4; Job 6:8). David prayed for a son to live, but he died (2 Sam. 12:16). A little reflection would show that God cannot grant some prayers. He may decline because He knows that to answer is not in our best interests. He may decline or delay the answer because He knows that to answer at a later time would bring Him greater glory and do the believer more good. I have thanked God many times that He did not answer some of my desires.

Generally, God denies our requests in prayer because of sin. Neglecting personal holiness will hinder our prayers. Psalm 66:18 says,

"If I regard iniquity in my heart, the Lord will not hear me." The psalmist is not talking about committing sin, but allowing sin to reign. The Lord told Isaiah concerning the nation of Israel, "Your iniquities have made a separation between you and your God, and your sins have hid his face from you so that he does not hear (answer)" (Isa. 59:2). Sin places a barrier in front of prayers. Persistent unconfessed sin strikes at the heart of effective prayer (Ps. 24:3-4).

There are several *specific areas* mentioned in the Bible that will affect God's response:

FAILURE TO PRAY – James 4:2d says, "You do not have because you do not ask." Unoffered prayers are unanswered prayers. We wonder why God doesn't answer more of our prayers, while God wonders why we don't pray more! Our Father is much more willing to answer our prayers than we are to ask of Him in prayer (James 1:5; Matt. 7:7-8). The crucial question for us to consider is not, "Does God answer prayer?" The question is, "Do I really pray?"

LACK OF FAITH – Some have not because they ask not. Others "have not" because they believe not. Doubt and unbelief are "prayer-stoppers" (Mk. 11:22, 24; cp. Matt. 21:22; James 1:5-8). Faith founded on the Word and in line with God's will is what really makes prayer work. A lack of trust in God is often the result of a lack of confidence in God Himself. We can approach the Father with bold confidence when we pray (Heb. 4:14-16).

FAILURE TO ABIDE IN THE WORD (John 15:7; 1 John 3:22) – It makes no sense to pray if we are not abiding in Christ and His Word is not abiding in us. There is a hand-in-hand relationship between the Word of God and prevailing prayer (Prov. 28:9). The Bible is the Christian's prayer book. If we abide in Him (union) and let His Word abide in us (communion), then we will pray consistently with His plan.

SELFISH CONCERNS AND MOTIVES (James 4:1-3) – If we become more concerned for ourselves than others, God will close His concern for us (Prov. 21:13). It makes no sense to pray with a selfish spirit. We need to continually examine our motives behind our prayers. Too often we bother God with our desires, rather than asking Him what He desires for us. Instead of being selfishly motivated, we should pray for God to be glorified (Matt. 5:16; 6:33; John 14:13). For examples of selfish praying, see Matthew 20:20-22; 23:14; Mark 12:40; Luke 20:47. What we ask for is really small compared to the glory God will receive. As you pray, learn to ask, "Is this petition for God's glory, for my good, and for the good of others, or is it merely to gratify my own selfish desires?"

REQUESTS THAT ARE TOO GENERAL – Prayer requests should be as specific as possible (Phil. 4:6; etc.). Sometimes we ask for everything in general and nothing in particular, such as, "Bless the sick, save the lost, etc." General prayers make it difficult to know if God ever answers. Praying that is effective must be definite, specific, and to the point. As someone once said, it should be "retail rather than whole-sale." We should avoid general requests for blanket blessings. Instead, we should make specific pleas for definite desires (Mark 11:24; Matt. 7:9-11; James 5:17-18).

FAMILY PROBLEMS (1 Pet. 3:7) – Mistreatment of family members is another hindrance to answered prayer. We should respect, honor, submit, and forgive one another. It only makes sense for Christian households to live by God's rules so that their prayers will not be hindered. Conflict in the home directly confuses the clear channel of God's answers to prayer.

UNFORGIVING ATTITUDE (Mark 11:24-26) – Jesus made it clear that forgiveness and prayer are inseparable. An unforgiving attitude renders prayer totally ineffective (Matt. 5:23-24). Making requests of God while refusing to forgive others is utter nonsense. A spirit of forgiveness should characterize every Christian (Eph. 4:32; Matt. 6:14-15; 18:35). No believer can stand on his platform of prayer if he has not learned how to forgive as well as to be forgiven. All too often do we seek blessings from the Father while at the same time abusing our relationships with others in His family.

CONFLICTS WITH HIS WILL (1 John 5:14-15). God delights in answering prayer that is consistent with His will. This is what it means to "pray in the Spirit" (Eph. 6:18; Jude 20) or to pray "in Jesus's name"

(John 14:13-14; 16:23-26). We can pray in the will of God only as we pray by the Word of God. The Holy Spirit will never lead us to pray for anything contrary to the written Word of God. Never forget that the purpose of prayer is to get God's will done. As we pray in the Spirit or in Jesus's name, we are only asking something because it is in character with the person and work of Jesus. We strive only to present prayers that He can endorse and approve.

LACK OF GENEROSITY (Prov. 21:13) – Prayer is oftentimes hindered by a stingy attitude. If we shut our ears in unconcern to the cry of those in need, in due time, we shall cry to God to only have Him deny our request (Prov. 19:17; 1 John 3:17-18). Stinginess in doing our part will hinder God from doing His part (Luke 6:38).

FAILURE TO PERSEVERE – Sometimes God denies our prayer requests because we are too impatient to wait on the Lord. The parables in Luke 11:5-10 and 18:1-8 teach us the shameless persistence God seeks in prayer. The New Testament abounds with the concept of perseverance in prayer (Rom. 12:12; Eph. 6:18; Col. 4:2; 1 Thess. 5:17). To persevere in prayer means to live your life in God-consciousness. Constant prayer is to be so God-conscious that you see all of life in reference to God. A persevering pray-er knows he can pray anywhere at any time. Prayer is not just an act; it is an attitude of life.

CONCLUSION: Sin robs prayer of its power. Prayer is only as powerful as the spiritual condition of the pray-er. Yes, God does answer prayer! Whatever His response, you can be sure it is in your best interest.

Chapter 9

HEARING GOD'S VOICE

Prayer is dialogue, not monologue. Effective communication with God includes speaking to God as well as listening to Him speak to us. The listening side of prayer is extremely important in developing a meaningful relationship with God.

God still speaks! The Bible says:

> Guard your steps when you go to the house of God; **to draw near to listen** is better than to offer the sacrifice of fools; for they do not know that they are doing evil. Be not rash with your mouth, nor let your heart be hasty to utter a word before God, for God is in heaven, and you upon earth; therefore, let your words be few. (Ecclesiastes. 5:1-2)

Solomon advises us to draw near to God and listen. The psalmist stated, "Let me hear what God the Lord will speak..." (Ps. 85:8). God Himself declared at the Transfiguration, "This is my Son, my chosen; **listen to Him!**" (Luke 9:35). Jesus Himself said, "My sheep hear my voice..." (John 10:27). For us to hear, He must be speaking. God's heart is that His people listen to Him (Ps. 81:8-16).

The problem today is not that God is no longer speaking, but rather that many are not listening. Robert Hale remarked, "God's still broadcasting, but most people are watching the game on another channel." There are several key *elements* in hearing God's voice.

I. WE SHOULD KNOW *HOW HE SPEAKS*

- **Biblical Times** – In biblical times, God spoke in various ways, which are stated in both the Old and New Testament. He spoke through:
  - *Direct Revelation* from His Spirit to man's spirit (Adam and Eve; Noah; Abraham; Moses; etc.).
  - *Dreams and Visions* (Gen. 15:1; 37:5-11; Dan. 2:1-3, 24-46; 7-12).
  - *His Word*, such as in the Ten Commandments (Exo. 20:1-17).
  - *His Prophets*, who were His mouthpiece (Elisha, Elijah, Isaiah, etc.).

- o *Circumstances*—Gideon is a good example of this (Judges 6:36-40).
- o *Angels* (Josh. 5:13-15; Gen. 16:7; 19:1; 22:11).
- o *The Holy Spirit* (Acts 2:4-12; 4:31).
- o *Jesus Christ* (Heb. 1:1-4).

- **After Bible Times** – How does God speak today? He uses various means to communicate. He speaks today through:
  - o *His Word.* Today God primarily speaks through His written and completed Word (2 Tim. 3:15-17). We need to learn to hear with our eyes as we read and study the Scriptures.
  - o *Others.* God also uses others to communicate to us. This person could be a relative, a friend, a pastor, or a total stranger. This person could be another Christian or even a lost person. God may speak through a passing conversation, a formal sermon, or in a counseling situation. He often uses books or tapes by others as well.
  - o *The Holy Spirit.* The Spirit of God searches and knows us (Ps. 139:23-24; 1 Cor. 2:11-16; Rom. 8:26-27). As He did to Elijah (1 Kings 19:11-13), God still speaks to us through "a still small voice" (Rom. 8:14-16).
  - o *Our Circumstances.* God not only speaks through people, but also through the circumstances of life. He communicates in our successes, and even more so in our failures. God speaks in times of temptation and difficulty, and He even speaks in those times of heartache and death. However, we

must be careful to know that circumstances alone do not determine God's will.

Whenever and however God speaks to us, whether through others, circumstances, or His Holy Spirit, He will always speak consistent with His revealed and written Word—no exceptions!

II. HE NEEDS *OUR ATTENTION*

If we are going to hear from God, He must have our undivided attention. All too often we are guilty of silencing the voice of God with our selfishness. As a result, we shut God out and do not give Him our attention. Because God loves us and desires to protect and bless us, He will do whatever is necessary to get our attention. There are many ways in which God aims to get our attention:[1]

- God may cause a **restless spirit** within us. Many times, God will use an uneasiness of heart, especially in life changing decisions (job, move, etc.), to speak to our spirit. An example of this is found in Esther 6, when King Ahasuerus could not sleep, and as a result, the whole Jewish nation was saved.
- Sometimes God gets our attention by **speaking through someone else.** God used Eli the priest to get young Samuel's ear for God (1 Sam. 3:1-14).
- When God **blesses us in an unusual way,** He can also get our attention. We would all like for God to get our attention

through pleasant circumstances, and Romans 2:4 indicates that God's goodness and kindness are intended to draw us closer to Him in repentance and faith.

- **Silence** is another means that God uses to get our attention. Sometimes, even when the prayer is in His will, God will close doors and be silent in an effort to make us stop and examine our lives. God denied David's prayer to spare his illegitimate child, but He certainly got David's attention (2 Sam. 12:15b-23).

- **Disappointments** in life are good ways for God to get our attention too. Whenever our world collapses, we usually become more receptive to listen to the voice of God. The disobedience of the Hebrew people prevented an entire adult generation from entering the Promised Land, and they were so disappointed (Num. 13-14). The next time disappointment comes, don't get angry or try to get even; instead, get attentive—God may be speaking!

- God will use **unusual circumstances** and experiences to get our attention. When Moses saw the burning bush that was not consumed, he stopped to ask why (Ex. 3:1-6). There are never any accidents for the child of God. The loving Father's sovereign hand guides the steps of His children. He allows and sends circumstances to cause us to stop and listen. Every believer should learn to look for God in every circumstance of life.

- God may choose to allow **failure** and **selfish presumption** to get our attention. On the heels of tremendous blessings and victory at Jericho (Josh. 6), the Hebrews were miserably humiliated at little Ai (Josh. 7). Why? They made two mistakes. First, Achan sinned by stealing some of the "booty" from Jericho, and secondly, they presumptuously tried to win with their own plans. But, listen—failing doesn't make you a failure. It can be used as a stepping stone to success if we allow God so speak to us through it.

- When **God dries up our resources**, especially financially, He can usually gain a listening ear. God perhaps uses this more than any other way to get our attention. In Judges 6:1-7, the Israelites only "cried to the Lord" for help after God had used the Midianites to deplete their material possessions.

- **Tragedy** is another means God employs to get our attention. God often allows tragedy in order to get our ear. The impatient grumbling of the Hebrew people brought many an early desert grave (Num. 21:4-6). After this, God had their attention (Num. 21:7-9).

- Another way God gets our attention is through **sickness** and **affliction**. King Hezekiah became ill as a result of a proud heart (2 Chron. 32:20-26). In his sickness, he listened to God. God struck the apostle Paul blind on the road to Damascus to get his attention (Acts 9:1-9).

God works uniquely with every believer. He knows exactly what it will take at a given time to get our attention. Every way God uses—be it none, one, or more of these "attention-getters"—He is merely expressing His love for His children. How we respond is crucial. The wise response is to ask, "Lord, what is it you're trying to say to me?" Then, when He speaks, obey!

III. WE MUST *RECOGNIZE HIS VOICE*

There are many voices crying for our attention today—the voices of self, others, church, family, vocation, Satan, and more. Recognizing God's voice should be normal and natural for a Spirit-filled Christian. Jesus told us in John 10:27, "My sheep hear my voice." (cp. John 10:3-5). However, there are times when recognizing the voice of God over that of self or this world is extremely difficult. There are several criteria to help us identify the voice of God. When God speaks, His voice will:

- **Be consistent with the written and completed Word.** We must always judge the voice we hear by what the Bible says. Neither God nor His truth ever change (1 John 3:24-4:6). Don't forget that God primarily speaks through the Scriptures. When the Bible speaks, God speaks. God will never lead us to say or do anything that contradicts His Word.
- **Often conflict with human wisdom.** It is no surprise that God's will often opposes man's wisdom (1 Cor. 1:17-2:5). Recognize that we should never place human reason over divine revelation.

- **Clash with selfish desires.** The voice of God would never lead us to say or do anything that would fulfill our fleshly, sinful desires. God will always move us to walk in the Spirit (Gal. 5:16-25).

- **Challenge my faith.** Satan wants to destroy our faith; God desires to develop it. The voice of God will always challenge faith to mature us.

- **Create courage in my life.** Many times, it will take courage and commitment to follow the voice of God. Satan deceptively makes life look easy and enjoyable. The voice of God will often demand great courage to obey.

- **Caution me to think of how others will be affected.** God is always concerned about others. He would never have us affect others harmfully. Our Lord would not encourage us to exercise "our rights" (Matt. 18:1-9; 1 Cor. 9:1-15). Satan whispers for us to go it alone. God shouts for us to care for one another.

- **Cause us to be patient.** Over and over, the Bible tells us to wait upon the Lord. Our world is an "instant" society. Satan pushes us to hurry up. The voice of God says that He is in control, so be patient. He is in no hurry.

- **Consider future consequences.** God's will is concerned for both now and then. He would not lead a believer to sacrifice the eternal on the altar of the temporal. Satan says to go for it all today. God's voice leads us to prepare for tomorrow.

- **Bring calm to your soul**. If God is not speaking, then peace won't come and remain. His voice gives peace that passes all human understanding (Phil. 4:7, 9; John 14:27).

- **Deepen commitment to obey the Lordship of Christ.** The voice of God speaks so that we can know Him better, love Him more, and follow Him completely. When God speaks, He will do so to make us more like Jesus Christ. If we are willing to follow the Lordship of Jesus, then God will speak to our hearts (John 7:17). As we obey His revealed will in His word, we develop a "listening ear."

CONCLUSION: God is still speaking—primarily through His Word. He desires to communicate to us much more than we desire to communicate with Him. He lovingly speaks to guide and comfort His children. When He speaks, we should respond with an attitude of submission, trust, and thanksgiving. Are you listening? Listen for His speaking in whatever season you may find yourself, and especially in the ordinary flow of life. Learn to "be still and know that I am God" (Ps. 46:10).

Chapter 10

PRAYING THROUGH PROBLEMS

Even Christians have problems. In fact, just becoming a committed Christian can create problems. How is a believer to deal with difficulty? Learning to pray through problems is crucial. Using King Jehoshaphat's experience as recorded in 2 Chronicles 20, we find some key principles for solving problems through prayer.

Jehoshaphat was a good and godly king who sought to reform the people. He reigned over Judah some twenty-five years (875-850 B.C.). In 2 Chronicles 20, Jehoshaphat faces an attack from an insurmountable foe. How he faced his problem provides some necessary principles for solving problems through prayer.

I. Accept God's solution, whatever it is, before a problem arises (vv. 1-3).

When praying through a problem, we should never come to God with some predetermined answer in our mind as to how God should resolve our problem. Regardless of the nature of a problem, it is essential that we accept God's solution no matter what.

II. Believe that our heavenly Father is vitally and personally interested in our problem (v. 4).

Like Jehoshaphat, so it is with every believer. Upon conversion, we enter into a covenant relationship with God. Every need and desire we have matters to our Father. **Every problem we have is God's problem** (v.15). We must realize that God can and will be involved with us in our problem.

III. Affirm that God is greater than our problem (vv. 5-7).

Jehoshaphat prayed and praised the sovereign power of God. **There is nothing we'll ever face that is greater than our God. No problem is too big for God!** This kind of affirmation will provide great confidence in any difficulty. God is never confused by or subject to any problem we'll ever face.

IV. Seek the Lord first (vv. 1-4).

Twice the passage says that Jehoshaphat sought the Lord for help (vv. 3-5). Even though he was much afraid (v. 3), when the problem came, his first response was to seek the Lord in prayer. **Seeking the Lord should always be my initial response to every problem.** Too often we're in a hurry to solve the problem our way. We must give God the time and attention necessary for Him to sift our fearful thoughts and replace them with His.

V. Realize that God may want us to involve others in praying about our problem (vv. 3-5).

Jehoshaphat encouraged all of Judah to join him in fasting and seeking the Lord. Many of life's problems are resolved between us and God alone. Yet, in some problems, it is God's plan for others to become involved. Why? First, God does not want us to become self-sufficient islands. Second, others can learn from our struggles. Third, we need the support of intercessory prayer.

VI. Believe that God will provide the answer to our problem (vv. 12-20).

Our heavenly Father is in the problem-solving business. He always knows what to do about every problem we face. He does not need our help. He will answer our problem either directly or indirectly. In Jehoshaphat's case, God spoke the solution through Jahaziel (vv.13-17). But remember, **God's answer is not always what we expect.** We should neither fear nor fight our problem. We must know that He has the answer. He is working in and through our every problem. Many times, God will provide a specific passage of Scripture that applies directly to our problem.

VII. Keep our praying God-centered rather than problem-centered (vv. 6-12).

Jehoshaphat's prayer is clearly focused on the person and promises of God. We should concentrate our attention on God and His faithfulness rather than on us and our problems.

VIII. God's solution usually demands a step of obedient faith (vv. 21-23).

Most of the time, we want God to solve our problems and demand nothing of us. God does not oftentimes work this way. He may require some risk-taking on our part. We must learn to live by faith. There are those times when risk overrides reason and faith overrides fear. In Jehoshaphat's problem, God's solution was to have the choir lead the army, and the weapons were songs of praise!

IX. God will give peace and rest about our problem (vv. 29-30).

If we listen and obey, then God will work. He may not always remove the problem, but He will give us peace in it.

X. God will use our problem and response to influence others (v. 29).

Because Jehoshaphat listened and obeyed, "the fear of God came on all the kingdoms of the countries..." How you and I work through the difficulties of life has a profound effect on the cause of Christ.

CONCLUSION: Whenever we try to solve problems by our own means and in our own timing, then disaster is just ahead. Instead, we must learn to come to our heavenly Father in humble and submissive prayer—affirming God for who He is, acknowledging our relationship with Him, and accepting His solution, whatever it is. Then we must move out in faith. In time, He will either remove our problem or give us the grace to see it through.

Chapter 11

PUTTING IT ALL TOGETHER

The A-C-T-S plan has helped me. It is a workable template. We must be careful not to get so caught in the outline that we fail to foster the relationship.

How does it all come together? How do we join adoration, confession, thanksgiving, intercession, petition, and hearing God's voice in a concentrated time of prayer? Certainly not all of these elements are included in every prayer, yet they should all be included in a normal time of prayer. You may ask, "Are there some keys to help me effectively communicate with God? How can I organize and experience a meaningful time of being alone with God?" Let me suggest some key factors and practical procedures for developing and maintaining moments with God.

I. DESIRE in your heart to have personal time with God through His Word and in prayer. This is where it starts. If we don't desire time alone with God, then procedure offers little help. First, we need to be motivated, and then the method comes. Ask God to place in you an insatiable desire for Him and His Word. Pray for God to make you hungry and thirsty for Him. Read the following passages: Matthew 5:6; Psalm 42:1-2; 63:1; 143:6.

II. DEFINE a particular time and place for your time alone with God. Morning is typically best, since the entire day is ahead of you. In Matthew 6:5, our Lord says, "when you pray, go into your room and shut the door and pray to your Father..." This indicates that there is a "when" of prayer. If you have this time in the morning, then be sure to remember these things: get to bed, get your rest, set your alarm, and get up. You have an important meeting with God. This verse further suggests there's a place of prayer, which should be a place that is quiet and private.

III. DISCIPLINE yourself for some reading of God's Word. Ask the Father to "open your eyes so you can see the wonderful things in His Word" (Ps. 119:18). Discipline yourself to read:

- Regularly – Daily reading is essential (Acts 17:11). Develop the habit of regular time in God's Word.
- Systematically – Systematically read through the Bible. Avoid random reading.
- Repeatedly – Using the same translation (version), reread the same portion of Scripture for several days (Isa. 28:10, 13). This

will help you have a "mental picture" of where a passage is and also what it says.

- Obediently – God's Word best works when it is applied. The primary purpose of Bible study is to change our lives (Titus 1:2; 2:10; 1 John 2:3-6). Always relate truths you have learned to life. The following acronym (SPACE) will aid in meditation for application:

  S – Is there any Sin for me to forsake (ex: bad attitudes or impure motives)?

  P – Is there any Promise, Assurance, or New Truth from God for me to believe? As we search for the promises, we need to see and think through their conditions too.

  A – Is there any Action or Error (in doctrine) for me to avoid?

  C – Is there a Command for me to obey?

  E – Is there an Example for me to follow (or avoid)?

- Recordingly – Write down selective and specific truths and applications the Lord gave you. Always make it personal.

- Memorize portions of Scripture. Memorization is an essential tool to help you know God's Word better.

IV. **DEVOTE** yourself to prayer. After God has spoken to you through His Book, then speak and listen to Him in prayer. Using the **A-C-T-S** acronym, spend time in prayer.

A – Adoration and praise. Reflect on who God is. Praise Him for His love, faithfulness, holiness, power, etc. Read some from the book of Psalms. You may even sing a little bit! The following list of praise scriptures, the names of God, and the attributes of God can be used as a resource for praising and expressing adoration to God.

Praise Scriptures

Psalm 100:4: "Enter His gates with thanksgiving and His courts with praise. Give thanks to Him and bless His name."

Psalm 150:2, 6: "Praise Him for His mighty deeds. Praise Him according to His excellent greatness. ... Let everything that hath breath praise the Lord."

Psalm 18:46: "The Lord lives, and blessed be my rock, and exalted be the God of my salvation."

Psalm 62:6: "He only is my rock and my salvation. My stronghold, I shall not be shaken."

Psalm 95:1: "O come, let us sing for joy to the Lord. Let us shout joyfully to the rock of our salvation."

Psalm 113:3: "From the rising of the sun to its setting, the name of the Lord is to be praised."

Proverbs 30:5: "Every word of the Lord is tested. He is a shield to those who take refuge in Him."

Isaiah 40:8: "The grass withers, the flower fades, but the word of our God stands forever."

Isaiah 40:31: "Yet those who wait for the Lord will gain new strength. They will mount up with wings like eagles. They will run and not get tired. They will walk and not grow weary."

1 Chronicles 29:10-13: "So David blessed the Lord in the sight of all the assembly; and David said, "Blessed art Thou, O Lord God of Israel our father forever and ever. Thine O Lord is the greatness and the power and the glory and the victory and the majesty, indeed everything that is in the heavens and the earth; Thine is the dominion, O Lord, and Thou doest exalt Thyself as head over all. Both riches and honor come from Thee and Thou doest rule over all, and in Thy hand is power and might and it lies in Thy hand to make great and

to strengthen everyone. Now therefore, our God, we thank Thee and praise Thy glorious name."

1 Kings 8:23: "O Lord, the God of Israel, there is no God like Thee in heaven above or on earth beneath who art keeping covenant and showing loving kindness to Thy servants who walk before Thee with all their heart."

Exodus 15:2, 11: "The Lord is God and I will praise Him. My Father is God and I will exalt Him. Who is like Thee, majestic in holiness, awesome in praises, working wonders?"

Isaiah 42:6: "I am the Lord, I have called you in righteousness; I will also hold you by the hand and watch over you."

Isaiah 43:13: "Even from eternity I am He; And there is no one who can deliver out of My hand. I act and who can reverse it?"

Isaiah 40:28: "The Everlasting God, the Lord, the Creator of the ends of the earth does not become weary or tired. His understanding is inscrutable. He gives strength to the weary."

Psalm 150:1, 2, 6: "Praise God in His sanctuary; Praise Him in His mighty expanse. Praise Him for His mighty deeds; Praise Him according to His excellent greatness. ... Let everything that has breath praise the Lord. Praise the Lord!"

Jeremiah 32:18, 19: "Oh great and mighty God, the Lord of Hosts is His name; Great in counsel and might in deed, whose eyes are open to all the ways of the sons of man, giving to everyone according to His ways and according to the fruit of His deeds."

Revelation 15:3, 4: "Great and marvelous are Thy works, O Lord God, the Almighty; Righteous and true are Thy ways, Thou King of the nations. Who will not fear, Oh Lord, and glorify Thy name? For Thou alone art holy; For all the nations will come and worship before Thee, for Thy righteous acts have been revealed."

2 Samuel 22:31-34: "As for God, His way is blameless; The word of the Lord is tested; He is a shield to all who take refuge in Him. For who is God besides the Lord? And who is a rock besides our God? God is my strong fortress and He sets the blameless in His way. He makes my feet like hinds' feet, and sets me on my high places."

Isaiah 45:6: "There is no one besides Me. I am the Lord, and there is no other."

Philippians 4:19: "And my God shall supply all your needs according to His riches in glory in Christ Jesus."

Additional Praise Scriptures

2 Samuel 22:1-4, 47, 50, 51; Exodus 15:1-18; Psalm 24:110, 8:1-2; 9:1-2, 7, 11; 16:7-9, 18:1-2; 34:1-3; 41:13; 48:1; 61:8; 67:3-5; 71:8; 103:1-2; 119:171-172; 119:164; 147:1; Romans 11:33-36; Ephesians 1:3; 3:20-21; 1 Peter 2:9; Revelation 15:3-4; 19:4-7

Names of God

Elohim – "One who is great, mighty, and dreadful"

El Shaddai – "God Almighty"

Adonai – "Lord"

YHWH (Yahweh/Jehovah) – "I AM"

Jehovah-Jireh (Gen. 22:14) – "The Lord provides"

Jehovah-Rophe (Ex. 15:26) – "The Lord heals"

Jehovah-Nissi (Ex. 17:15) – "The Lord our Banner"

Jehovah-M'Kaddesh (Lev. 20:8) – "The Lord who sanctifies"

Jehovah-Shalom (Judg. 6:24) – "The Lord our Peace"

Jehovah-Rohi (Ps. 23:1) – "The Lord my Shepherd"

Jehovah-Tsidkenu (Jer. 23:5-6) – "The Lord our Righteousness"

Jehovah-Shammah (Ezek. 48:35) – "The Lord is present"

Attributes of God

Omniscient – God knows all. He has perfect knowledge of everything that is past, present, or future (Job 37:1; Ps. 139:1-6).

Omnipotent – God possesses all power. He is able to bring into being anything He has decided to do, with or without the use of any means (Gen. 18:14; Job 42:2; Jer. 32:27).

Omnipresent – God is present everywhere, in all the universe, at all times, in the totality of His character (Prov. 15:3; Jer. 23:23-24).

Eternal – God has no beginning, and He has no end. He is not confined to the finiteness of time or man's reckoning of time. He is, in fact, the cause of time (Deut. 32:40; Isa. 57:15).

Immutable – God is always the same in His nature, His character, and His will. He never changes, and He can never be made to change (Ps. 102:25-27; Mal. 3:6; Heb. 13:8).

Incomprehensible – Because God is God, He is beyond the understanding of man. His ways, acts, and character are higher than ours. We only understand as He chooses to reveal (Job 11:7; Isa. 55:8-9; Rom. 11:33).

Self-existent – There is nothing upon which God depends for His existence except Himself. The whole basis of His existence is within Himself. He added nothing to Himself by creation (Ex. 3:14; John 5:26).

Self-sufficient – Within Himself, God is able to act—to bring about His will without any assistance. Although He may choose to use assistance, it is His choice, not His need (Ps. 50:7-12; Acts 17:24-25).

Infinite – The realm of God has no limits or boundaries (1 Kings 8:27; Ps. 145:3).

Transcendent – God is above His creation, and He would exist if there were no creation. His existence is totally apart from His creatures or creation. (Isa. 43:10 and 55:8, 9).

Sovereign – God is totally, supremely, and preeminently over all His creation. There is not a person or thing that is not under His control or foreknown plan (Dan. 4:35).

Holy – God is a morally excellent, perfect being. His purity of being is in every aspect (Lev. 19:2; Job 34:10; Isa. 47:4; Isa. 57:15).

Righteous – God is always good. It is essential to His character. He always does the right thing. Ultimately, since He is God, whatever He does is right. He is the absolute. His actions are always consistent to His character, which is love (Deut. 32:4; Ps. 119:142).

Just – In all of His actions, God acts with fairness. Whether He deals with man, angels, or demons, He acts in total equity by rewarding righteousness and punishing sin. Since He knows all, every decree is absolutely just (Num. 14:18; 23:19; Ps. 89:14).

Merciful – God is an actively compassionate being. In His actions, He responds in a compassionate way toward those who have opposed His will in their pursuit of their own way (Ps. 62:12; 89:14; 116:5; Rom. 9:14-16).

Longsuffering – God's righteous anger is slow to be kindled against those who fail to listen to His warnings or obey His instructions. The eternal longing for the highest good for His creatures holds back His holy justice (Num. 14:18; 2 Peter 3:9).

Wise – God's actions are based on His character, which allows Him to choose righteous ends and make fitting plans to achieve those ends (Isa. 40:28; Dan. 2:20).

Loving – This attribute of God causes Him to give Himself for another, even to the laying down of His own life. This attribute causes Him to desire the other's highest good without any thought for Himself. This love is not based upon the worth, response, or merit of the object being loved (Jer. 31:3; Rom. 5:8; 1 John 4:8).

Good – This attribute of God causes Him to give to others in a way which has no motive and is not limited by what the recipients deserve (2 Chron. 5:13; Ps. 106:1).

Wrathful – There is within God a hatred for all that is unrighteous and an unquenchable desire to punish all unrighteousness (Ex. 34:6-7; 2 Chron. 19:2; Rom. 1:18).

Truthful – All that God says is reality. Whether man believes it or not, whether man sees it as reality or not, if God has spoken it, it is reality. Whatever He speaks becomes truth as we know it (Ps. 35:1; Titus 1:2).

Faithful – God is always true to His promises. He can never draw back from His promises of blessing or of judgment. Since He cannot lie, He is totally steadfast to what He has spoken (Deut. 7:9; 2 Tim. 2:13).

Jealous – God is unwilling to share His glory with any other creature or give up His redeemed people (Ex. 20:5; 34:14).

We can turn these attributes of God and names of God into first-person, personal statements about the God we adore. "God, I thank You that You are . . ." We can implement the praise scriptures as prayers or as springboards in our own expression of adoration.

C – Confession of sin. Having entered His holy presence through praise, you need to confess every known sin (Ps. 139:23-24; Ps. 66:18; 1 John 1:9). Ask God to bring to mind anything that needs to be confessed. When thoughts come to mind of past sins you have already sincerely confessed, realize that the enemy is trying to make you feel guilty. Simply stand on the truth that as far as the east is from the west, so far has God removed that sin from you, and He remembers it no more; so, you can't go there! (Ps. 103:11-12; Isa. 38:17; Mic. 7:19; Jer. 31:34). Be sensitive to attitudinal sins. Remember, the goal is to think like Jesus, so you will act like Jesus, or as Paul stated in 2 Corinthians 10:5, "Take every thought captive to the obedience of Christ."

Read "Questions for Personal Revival" in Appendix B for questions that may be helpful in assessing sinful attitudes and actions that may need to be confessed. It is important that we confess sin prior to interceding because Isaiah 59:2 tells us that "your sins have hidden His face from you, so that He does not hear." It is important to note that genuine biblical confession is always accompanied by repentance, which is a turning from the sin confessed.

T – Thanksgiving gives you a chance to express gratitude to God for what He has done in your life (Eph. 5:20; 1 Thess. 5:18; Phil. 4:6; Ps. 92:1; 116:12, 17). Try thanking God each day for:

- One *physical* blessing
- One *material* blessing
- One *people* blessing
- One *spiritual* blessing

S – Supplication has two parts:

Intercession for others. It is both a responsibility and a privilege to pray for others (1 Sam. 12:23; Eph. 1:15-19; 3:14-19). Pray more for spiritual blessings than material. Pray for the lost, those in places of leadership, the sick, the troubled, missions, and so on. Here are some spiritual blessings we can pray for one another:

Inner Spiritual Strength

Colossians 1:11: "Strengthened with all power, according to His glorious might for the attaining of all steadfastness and patience, joyously."

Ephesians 3:16: "I pray that God would grant you, according to the riches of His glory, to be strengthened in power through His Spirit in the inner man."

Divine Power/Realization of Spiritual Wealth

Ephesians 1:17-23: "That the God of our Lord Jesus Christ, the Father of glory, may give to you a spirit of wisdom and of revelation in the knowledge of Him. I pray that the eyes of your heart may be enlightened, so that you may know what is the hope of His calling, what are the riches of His inheritance in the saints, And what is the surpassing greatness of His power toward us who believe. These are in accordance with the working of the strength of His might which He brought about in Christ when He raised Him from the dead."

Abounding Love for Others

Ephesians 3:17-19: "So that Christ may dwell in your hearts through faith; and that you, being rooted and grounded in love, may be able to comprehend with all of the saints what is the breadth and length and height and depth; and to know the love of Christ which surpasses knowledge, that you may be filled up to all the fullness of God."

Philippians 1:9-11: "And this I pray that your love would abound still more and more in real knowledge and all discernment, so that you may approve the things that are excellent, in order to be sincere and blameless on the day of judgment, having been filled with the fruit of righteousness which comes through Jesus Christ to the glory and praise of God."

Effective Witness

Acts 4:29: "Lord . . . grant that Thy bond-servants may speak Thy word with all confidence."

Daily Sustenance

Philippians 4:19: "My God shall supply all your needs according to His riches in glory in Christ Jesus."

Psalm 34:10: "They who seek the Lord shall not be in want of any good thing."

Contentment in Circumstances

Philippians 4:11: "I have learned to be content in whatever circumstances I am in."

Supernatural Wisdom

Colossians 1:9-10: "That you may be filled with the knowledge of His will in all spiritual wisdom and understanding, so that you may walk in a manner worthy of the Lord, to please Him in all respects, bearing fruit in every good work and increasing in the knowledge of God."

James 1:5: "If any of you lacks wisdom, let him ask God, who gives generously to all without reproach, and it will be given him."

1 Corinthians 2:16: "For who has understood the mind of the Lord so as to instruct him?" But we have the mind of Christ."

Moral Purity

Titus 2:11: "Deny ungodliness and worldly desires and to live sensibly, righteously and godly in the present age."

2 Timothy 2:22: "Now flee from youthful lusts, and pursue righteousness, faith, love and peace with those who call upon the Lord from a pure heart."

1 Timothy 4:7: "Discipline yourself for the purpose of godliness."

Knowledge of God

Philippians 3:10, 14: "That I may know Him and the power of His resurrection and the fellowship of His sufferings, being conformed to His death. ... I press on toward the goal for the prize of the upward call of God in Christ Jesus."

Unity

John 17:21: "That they may all be one; even as Thou, Father, art in Me, and I in Thee, that they also may be in Us, that the world may believe that Thou didst send me."

Salvation of the Lost

2 Peter 3:9: "The Lord is...not wishing for any to perish but for all to come to repentance."

Spirit-filled, Spirit-led, bearing fruit of the Spirit

Ephesians 5:10: "Be filled with the Spirit. "And try to discern what is pleasing to the Lord."

Galatians 5:18: "But if you are led by the Spirit, you are not under the law."

Galatians 5:22: "But the fruit of the Spirit is love, joy, peace, patience, kindness, goodness, faithfulness, gentleness, self-control."

Petition for yourself. There is nothing wrong with praying for yourself as long as you keep it in perspective (Matt. 7:7-11; James 4:1-3). As you pray, be sure to submit your life totally to God, put on the whole armor of God, and seek God's wisdom throughout the day. We have our armor on when we are *living* what each piece represents. If you sin, you have taken off the breastplate of righteousness; if you panic when your trial comes, you have taken down the shield of faith, etc. However, going over the pieces in prayer reminds us of what we are to be doing throughout our day. See page 62 for a prayer to put on the whole armor of God.

There are so many needs to pray for that it is helpful to categorize the types of needs you will pray for and assign them to different days of the week. For example:

- Monday: Family
- Tuesday: Self, Ministry, Work, etc.
- Wednesday: Friends
- Thursday: Local, State, and Federal Governmental Leaders
- Friday: The Lost
- Saturday: Revival in America
- Sunday: Church Leaders, Worship Services

You will be your best for God if you strive to meet with Him regularly. I warn you that establishing and maintaining your time alone with God will not be easy. You will have to relentlessly guard this time if you are to keep it. The whole time you are praying, be sure to give

God a listening ear. He is speaking. The question is: Are you listening and obeying?

EPILOGUE

In many ways, prayer is still a mystery to me and others for sure. Jesus is still teaching me to pray. The ACTS acronym has provided a helpful guide in my conversations with God. Perhaps, you will find it helpful too. Each must find what works for them. As stated earlier in the book, we must always be very careful not to get so caught up in whatever guide we use and fail to foster a growing conversation and relationship with our heavenly Father. Our commitment must be this: When the Bible teaches principles of prayer, God expects us to obey. Our response is not to reason why, but simply to obey. G. Campbell Morgan said, "Any discussion of prayer which did not issue in the practice of prayer is not only not helpful but dangerous." Developing a meaningful prayer life is essential to living an abundant Christian life. Learning to pray does not come easy. It takes knowledge, patience, and work. Join me in praying, "Lord, teach me to pray!"

ENDNOTES

Introduction

1. Samuel D. Gordon, *Quiet Talks on Prayer* (Westwood, NJ: The Christian Library, 1984), 11.

2. Dick Eastman, *The Hour That Changes the World* (Grand Rapids: Baker Book House, 1978), 17.

Chapter 1 "What Is 'Prayer'?"

1. Barry Wood, *Questions Christians Ask about Prayer and Intercession* (Old Tappan, NJ: Flaming H. Revel, 1984), 15.

Chapter 2 "Why Pray at All?"

1. Terry L. Miethe, *A New Christian's Guide to Following Jesus* (Minneapolis: Bethany House Pub., 1984), 86.

2. Leonard Ravenhill, *A Treasury of Prayer – The Best of E. M. Bounds* (Minneapolis, MN: Bethany House Pub., 1891), 36.

3. Jack R. Taylor, *Prayer: Life's Limitless Reach* (Nashville: Broadman Press, 1977), 42.

4. Jack McAlister, *Change the World School of Prayer*: 2d. ed.; (Studio City, CA: World Literature Crusade, 1978), A 18-21.

5. Ibid., 2.

6. Ibid., D 114.

7. Ibid., A 13.

8. Lehman Strauss, *Sense and Nonsense about Prayer* (Chicago: Moody Press 1978), 104-115.

9. McAlister, op. cit., C 58.

10. Ibid., A 12.

11. *The Kneeling Christian* (Grand Rapids: Zondervan Publishing House, 1971), 12.

Chapter 3 "Let's Begin with Adoration"

1. Eastman, op. cit, 25.

2. Taylor, op. cit., 71-102.

3. Eastman, op. cit., 22-23.

4. Taylor, op. cit., 17.

5. Ibid., 116.

Chapter 4 "Continue in Confession"

1. Alan Richardson, *A Theological Word Book of the Bible* (New York: Macmillian Pub. Co., 1950), 51-52.

2. Vines, op. cit., 216.

3. Strauss, op. cit., 24.

4. Eastman, op. cit., 44.

Chapter 5 "Try Thanksgiving"

1. John MacArthur, Jr. Study notes in Eph. 5:18-21, 51.
2. O. Hallesby, *Prayer* (Minneapolis: Augsburg Pub. House, 1959), 141.
3. Strauss, op. cit., 58.

Chapter 6 "Conclude in Supplication"

1. Eastman, op. cit., 158ff.
2. J.I. Packer, *Evangelism & the Sovereignty of God* (Downers Grove: Intervarsity Press, 1991), 11-12.

Chapter 7 "Winning the War though Prayer"

1. Bubek, *Raising Lambs among Wolves* (Chicago: Moody Press, 1997), 138.

Chapter 8 "Does God Answer Prayer?"

1. McAlister, op. cit., C 55.

Chapter 9 "Hearing God's Voice"

1. Charles Stanley, *How to Listen to God* (Nashville: Thomas Nelson Pub., 1985), 31-48.
2. Ibid., 51-63.

APPENDIX A

"Spiritual Warfare Prayers"

Prayer for Fighting Temptation (adapted from Mark Bubeck's "Raising Lambs Among Wolves," 138)

Heavenly Father, my old fleshly nature is tempting me to (name the temptation, i.e., lust, fear, resentment, anger, gossip), and I know that if it's left to itself, it is wicked enough to cause me to sin against You.

I affirm that through the work of Your cross I am dead with you to the rule and control of my flesh and its desire to (name of fleshly temptation being experienced at that moment, i.e., anger, lust, etc.).

Finally, heavenly Father, I ask You now to replace this fleshly desire that is tempting me to be (state the fleshly appeal, i.e. angry, lusting, jealous, etc.) with the fruit of Your control. Put within my mind, will, emotions, and body Your love, joy, peace, patience, and all the virtues that my Lord Jesus Christ enables me to live out for His glory.

Prayer of Renunciation and Affirmation (adapted from Mark Bubeck's "The Adversary," 148)

(None of us know what works of Satan may have been passed on to us from our ancestors. Therefore, it is wise for every child of God to make the following declaration and to repeat it from time to time. Speak it aloud, inserting your full name in the blank space.)

As a child of God, purchased by the blood of the Lord Jesus Christ, I _____, here and now renounce and repudiate all the sins of my ancestors. As one who has been delivered from the power of darkness and transferred into the kingdom of God's dear Son, I cancel out all demonic working that has been passed on to me from my ancestors.

As one who has been crucified with Jesus Christ and raised to walk in newness of life, I cancel every curse that may have been put upon me. I announce to Satan and all his hosts that Christ became a curse for me when He hung upon the Cross. As one who has been crucified and raised with Christ and now sits with Him in heavenly places, I renounce any and every way in which Satan may claim ownership of me. I declare myself to be completely and eternally signed over and committed to the Lord Jesus Christ.

All this I do on the basis of the truths revealed in the Scriptures and in the Name and on the authority of the Lord Jesus Christ (Eph. 1:7; 2:5-6; Col. 1:13; 1 John 3:8b; Gal. 2:20; 3:13; Rom. 6:4).

Prayer for a Loved One or Friend (adapted from Mark Bubeck's "The Adversary," 112)

Heavenly Father, I bring before You and the Lord Jesus Christ one who is very dear to You and to me, _____. I have come to see that Satan is blinding and binding him in awful bondage. He is in such a condition that he cannot or will not come to You for help on his own. I stand in for him in intercessory prayer before Your throne. I draw upon the Person of the Holy Spirit, that He may guide me to pray in wisdom, power, and understanding.

In the name of the Lord Jesus Christ, I loose _____ from awful bondage the powers of darkness are putting upon him. I bind all powers of darkness set on destroying his life. I bind them aside in the name of the Lord Jesus Christ and forbid them to work. I bind up all powers of depression that are seeking to cut _____ off and imprison him in a tomb of despondency. I bring in prayer the focus of the person and work of the Lord Jesus Christ directly upon _____ to his strengthening and help. I bring the mighty power of my Lord's incarnation, crucifixion, resurrection, ascension, and glorification directly against all forces of darkness seeking to destroy _____. I ask the Holy Spirit to apply all of the mighty work of the Lord Jesus Christ directly against all forces of darkness seeking to destroy _____.

I pray, heavenly Father, that You may open _____'s eyes of understanding. Remove all blindness and spiritual deafness from his

117

heart. As a priest of God in ____'s life, I plead Your mercy over his sins of failure and rebellion. I claim all of his life united together in obedient love and service to the Lord Jesus Christ. May the Spirit of the Living God focus His mighty work upon _____ to grant him repentance and to set him completely free from all that binds him.

In the name of the Lord Jesus Christ, I thank You for Your answer. Grant me the grace to be persistent and faithful in my intercessions for _____, that You may be glorified through this deliverance. Amen.

APPENDIX B

"Questions for Personal Revival" (Adapted from Pamphlet, Bibles for the World)

1. (Matt. 6:12-14) Is there anyone against whom you hold a grudge? Anyone you have not forgiven? Anyone you hate? Are there any misunderstandings that you are unwilling to forget? Is there any person against whom you are harboring bitterness, resentment, or jealousy? Anyone you dislike to be well spoken of or hear praised? Do you allow anything to justify a wrong attitude toward another?

2. (Matt. 6:33) Is there anything in which you have failed to put God first? Have your decisions been made by your own wisdom and desires, rather than by seeking and following God's will? Do any of the following in any way interfere with your surrender and service to God: ambition, pleasures, loved ones, friendships, desire for recognition, money, or your own plans?

3. (Mark 16:15) Have you failed to seek the lost for Christ? Have you failed to consistently witness with your mouth for the Lord Jesus Christ? Has your life not shown the Lord Jesus to the lost?

4. (John 13:35) Are you secretly pleased over the misfortunes of others? Are you secretly annoyed over the accomplishments or advancements of another? Are you guilty of any contention or strife? Do you quarrel, argue, or engage in heated discussions? Are there people whom you deliberately slight?

5. (Acts 20:35) Have you robbed God by withholding from Him the time, talents, and money He is due? Have you given less than a tenth of your income for God's work? Have you failed to support mission work either in prayer or in offerings?

6. (1 Cor. 4:2) Are you undependable so that you cannot be trusted with responsibilities for the Lord's work? Are you allowing your emotions to be stirred for the things of the Lord but doing nothing about it?

7. (1 Cor. 6:19-20) Are you in any way careless with your body? Do you fail to care for it as the temple of the Holy Spirit? Are you guilty of overeating or drinking? Are you adhering to the biblical standard of sexual purity outside of marriage or are you allowing the culture to influence you?

8. (1 Cor. 10:31) Do you take the slightest credit for anything good about you, rather than give all the glory to God? Do you talk of what you have done rather than of what Christ has done? Do your

statements mostly focus on "I"? Are your feelings easily hurt? Have you made a pretense of being something that you are not?

9. (Eph. 3:20) Are you self-conscious rather than Christ-conscious? Do you allow feelings of inferiority to keep you from attempting things you should do in service for God?

10. (Eph. 4:28) Do you underpay? Have you been careless in the payment of your debts? Have you sought to evade payment of your debts? Do you do very little in your work? Do you waste time? Do you waste the time of others?

11. (Eph. 4:31) Do you complain? Do you find fault? Do you have a critical attitude toward any person or anything? Do you get angry? Do you become impatient with others? Are you ever harsh or unkind? Are you irritable or cranky? Do you ever carry hidden anger?

12. (Eph. 5:16) Do you ask yourself, "Would Jesus watch this or listen to this" when choosing music, movies, etc.? Do you find it necessary to seek satisfaction from any questionable source? Are you doing certain things that show that you are not satisfied in the Lord Jesus Christ?

13. (Eph. 5:20) Have you neglected to thank God for all things—the seemingly bad as well as the good? Have you virtually called Him a liar by doubting His Word? Do you worry? Is your spiritual temperature based on your feelings instead of on the facts of God's Word?

14. (Phil. 1:21) Are you taken up with the cares of this life? Is your conversation or heart joyful over things rather than the Lord and

His Word? Does anything mean more to you than living for and pleasing God?

15. (Phil. 2:14) Do you ever seek to hurt someone through word or deed? Do you gossip? Do you speak unkindly concerning people when they are not present? Do you carry prejudice against true Christians because they are of some different group than yours, or because they do not see everything exactly like you?

16. (Phil. 4:4) Have you neglected to seek to be pleasing to Him in all things? Do you carry any bitterness toward God? Have you complained against Him in any way? Have you been dissatisfied with His provision for you? In your heart, is there any unwillingness to obey God fully? Do you have any reservations as to what you would or would not do concerning anything that might be His will? Have you disobeyed some direct leading from Him?

17. (Col. 3:9) Do you take seriously what comes out of your mouth? Do you ever lie? Do you ever exaggerate? Cheat? Steal?

18. (2 Tim. 2:22) Do you have any personal habits that are ungodly? Do you allow ungodly thoughts about the opposite sex to stay in your mind? Are your words intended to build others up?

19. (Heb. 10:25) Do you control your thoughts by kicking out those that do not line up with Scripture or are you allowing the culture to influence your thoughts and therefore your actions? Do you neglect to attend or participate in corporate worship? Have you neglected or slighted daily or private prayer? Have you neglected God's Word? Do you find the Bible and prayer uninteresting?

20. (Heb. 13:17) Do you hesitate to submit to leaders in the church or elsewhere? Are you lazy? Do you feel irritated when asked to serve at church or are you eager to be involved in service? Do you in any way have a stubborn or unteachable spirit?

21. (James 1:27) Have you allowed yourself to become "spotted" by the world? Is your manner of dress pleasing to God? Do you spend beyond what is pleasing to God on anything? Do you neglect to pray about the things you buy?

22. (James 4:6) Do you feel that you are doing quite well as a Christian? That you are not so bad? That you are good enough? Are you stubborn? Do you insist on having your own way? Do you insist on having your way over God's way?

23. (James 4:11) Have you dishonored God or hindered His work by criticizing His servants? Have you failed to pray regularly for your pastor or other spiritual leaders? Do you find it hard to be corrected? Are you more concerned about what people will think than what will be pleasing to God?

If you have been honest and true in the matter of admitting your sins, then you are ready for God's cleansing. Sins that are admitted are sins that are confessed. Remember these three things:

1. If the sin is against God, confess it to God, and make things right with God.

2. If the sin is against another person, confess it to God, and make the sin right with the other person.

3. If the sin is against a group, confess it to God, and make it right with the group.

If there is full confession, there will be full cleansing. Then the joy of the Lord will follow, and there can be testimony and prayer in the power of the Holy Spirit. Revival will follow.

Psalm 19:12— "Who can understand his errors? Cleanse thou me from secret faults."

SELECTED BIBLIOGRAPHY

Bubeck, Mark. *The Adversary*. Chicago: Moody Press, 1975.

_____. *Raising Lambs among Wolves*. Chicago: Moody Press, 1997.

Eastman, Dick. *The Hour That Changes the World*. Grand Rapids: Baker Book House, 1978.

Gordon, Samuel D. *Quiet Talks on Prayer*. Westwood NJ: The Christian Library, 1984.

Hallesby, O. *Prayer*. Minneapolis: Augsbarg Publishing House, 1959.

McAlister, Jack. *Change the World School of Prayer*. 2d ed.; Studio City, CA: World Literature Crusade, 1978.

Miethe, Terry L. *A New Christian's Guide to Following Jesus*. Minneapolis: Bethany House Publishers, 1984.

Ravenhill, Leonard. *A Treasury of Prayer – The Best of E.M. Bounds*. Minneapolis: Bethany House Publishers, 1891.

Taylor, Jack R. *Prayer: Life's Limitless Reach*. Nashville: Broadman Press, 1977

The Kneeling Christian. Grand Rapids: Zondervan Publishing House, 19741.

Richardson, Alan. *A Theological Word Book of the Bible*. New York: Macmillan Publishing Company, 1950.

Stanley, Charles. *How to Listen to God*. Nashville: Thomas Nelson Publishers, 1985.

Strauss, Lehman. *Sense and Nonsense about Prayer*. Chicago: Moody Press, 1978.

Vines, W.E. *An Expository Dictionary of Biblical Words*. Nashville: Thomas Nelson Publisher, 1984.

Wood, Barry. *Questions Christians Ask about Prayer and Intercession*. Old Tappan, NJ: Flaming H. Revell, 1984.

ABOUT THE AUTHOR

Since 1980, Jimmy has served on the staff at First Baptist Church of Orlando. A native Tennessean, Jimmy received his B.S. degree in Chemical Engineering at the University of Tennessee in 1973. Following God's call to vocational ministry, Jimmy earned his M.Div. in 1976 and his D.Min. in 2002, both from New Orleans Baptist Theological Seminary.

Jimmy is passionate about using his God-given talents and abilities to mature disciples and develop leaders. He is a gifted Bible teacher, leadership coach, and personal mentor. He has been privileged to teach leadership at college and seminary levels. He has authored several books, including *It's All about Leadership, Unwrapping God's Gifts to You*, and *Standing Tall When Tempted.*

Jimmy and his childhood sweetheart, Linda, married in 1973 and God has blessed them with four children and grandchildren as well. In his spare time, Jimmy loves to coach basketball, watch sports, read, and spend time with his outrageously wonderful grandchildren. Jimmy and Linda live in Orlando, Florida.

To learn more about Jimmy, follow him on JimmyKnott.com, LinkedIn, and Facebook.

CPSIA information can be obtained
at www.ICGtesting.com
Printed in the USA
FFHW010256020519
52205713-57578FF